Horses and Cattle, and a Double-Rigged Saddle

Horses and Cattle, and a Double-Rigged Saddle

Writings from the Western Range

Stephen Zimmer

Updated Edition

A Double Z Bar Ranch Book

Dedicated to the memory of my faithful

saddle horses, Mac and Will James.

Design, editing, and production: Steve Lewis.
Cover and frontispiece artwork: *"The Harderners"* by Keith Walters,
    Double Z Bar Ranch collection.

Library of Congress Control Number: 2021946085
ISBN: 978-0-9892807-5-4

ZZ   To contact the author:
    Double Z Bar Ranch
    230 Rayado Creek Road
    Cimarron, New Mexico 87714

Preface

"The daily life of the cowboy is so replete with privation, hardship, and danger that it is a marvel how any sane man can voluntarily assume it. Yet thousands of men not only do assume it, but actually like it to infatuation."

-- Richard Irving Dodge, 1882

"Tired horses and tired cowboys make the best ones."

-- Jiggs Porter, CS Ranch, Cimarron, New Mexico

The following collection of articles, stories, and essays represents forty years of interest in western ranch life and art. Most of what is included has been previously published in such magazines as *Western Horseman, Cowboy Magazine, Cowboys & Indians, Equine Art, Southwest Art, Persimmon Hill,* and *The Quarter Horse Journal.* My thanks to the editors of those periodicals for thinking that what I considered interesting about western life and people might be interesting to their readers as well.

One fact pertaining to the articles on cowboy material culture is that ranch men have always been slaves to fashion, just as much as women supposedly are. In reading memoirs and viewing photographs of cowpunchers in the old days, it is evident that they were much concerned with having the latest designs in saddles, stirrups, chaps, spurs, and bits. Similarly, after observing cowpunchers for the last thirty plus years, I can say that modern riders continue the trend.

Concerning western art, which is by nature realistic, cowboys and ranchers tend to view it primarily in terms its authenticity. Horses must run or stand naturally, bridles should hang properly, loops fly realistically, and hats must be creased as they would be seen on the range. A case in point is how I once heard a venerable old rancher comment on a painting that, although he approved of the scene of a rider roping a calf, he took exception to the artist's placement of the bridle buckle on the near side of the headstall, saying it was too close to the horse's eye.

Finally, I want to thank all of the cowboys and ranchers I've known over the years on ranches across Texas, New Mexico, and Arizona. I learned a lot from them, such as the value of hard work and the importance of keeping one's word. As an extra benefit I got to see some good country and ride a lot of good horses along the way.

Steve Zimmer
Double Z Bar Ranch
Cimarron, NM

Praise for
Horses and Cattle, and a Double-Rigged Saddle
by New Mexico ranch cowboys

"With his knowledge of the history of horses, cattle, and cowboys of the western range, Steve Zimmer has written a whole herd of true and authentic stories that anyone interested in things Western will not only like, but will also be able to learn from."

Doug Johnson
Philmont, UU Bar, TO, and WS Ranches

"This collection of stories of horses and people of the cow range is for anyone interested in authentic and accurate Western history, especially cowboys. Steve and I have ridden a lot of trails together, and I can tell you he knows his onions."

Rod Taylor
Philmont, UU Bar, TO, and WS Ranches

"I was raised on a New Mexico cow outfit and later rode for several big ones across the state. As you ride through Steve's book, you'll hear the nicker of ranch horses and the bawling of long horned cattle along with smelling the smoke of the cook's campfire and the whiff of a cowpuncher's Bull Durham cigarette."

Curtis Fort
Bell, Pitchfork, and WS Ranches

Contents

The Western Range Cattle Industry

The first ranches in North America were established by Franciscan friars at missions in northern Mexico during the 17th century. Cattle raising was the primary economic support for the missions, and the padres sustained themselves by trading in tallow and hides. They taught their Indian neophytes to ride horses in order to take care of the mission herds, thus making Indians the first cowboys. The cattle they herded descended from hardy Spanish Andalusian stock that had been imported into Mexico a century before, which eventually produced the fighting black bulls of Spain and Mexico and the hardy Longhorns of Texas.

The Franciscans expanded their missionary activity north into the province of Texas after 1690. They crossed the Rio Grande River with large herds of cattle and established several missions, the most important being San Antonio de Bexar. Eventually non-mission ranches, called *rancheros*, were built in Texas to use communal pastures and land grants bestowed by the King of Spain as cattle grazing lands.

Spanish cattle multiplied rapidly due to the favorable climate and range conditions in Texas. Invariably, many unbranded animals escaped from the missions and ranches. They were never claimed and became the foundation for herds of wild cattle in the region.

While mission ranches flourished in Texas, a Franciscan friar named Junipero Serra arrived in the Spanish province of California to establish missions along the Pacific coast. As in Texas, cattle were brought to the missions and Indians were trained to herd them. Hides and tallow were the primary commodities.

Catholic missionary activity in Texas ended in the 1790s. The mission herds were either taken over by the rancheros or abandoned to the open range. After Mexico gained its independence from Spain in 1821, numerous Americans emigrated to the province, drawn by land grants awarded by the Mexican government. Many of these Americans established cattle herds of their own. They learned horseback cattle handling from the Mexican *vaqueros* (cowboys) and as a result added many Spanish words to their vocabularies, such as corral, lasso, rancho, remuda, sombrero, and chaparejo.

In the northeastern provinces Americans banded together and fought for independence from Mexico, forming the Republic of Texas in 1836. As a result of the subsequent fighting, Mexican ranchers were forced south of the Rio Grande. Cattle abandoned to the open range joined the many thousands of animals already roaming there. At the time of the Texas Revolution it was estimated that there were six head of cattle in Texas for every Texan. Even though the supply of wild cattle was great, there were few markets for them aside from local consumption or for use as beasts of burden.

Typical Texas cattlemen of the time were described by a visiting Englishman in 1843 as "a rude, uncultivated race of beings who pass the greater part of their lives in the saddle, herding cattle and horses, and in hunting deer, buffalo, or mustangs. Unused to comfort and regardless of ease and danger, they have a hardy, brigand, sunburnt appearance... with a slouched hat, leather hunting shirt, leggings and Indian moccasins, armed with a large knife, musket or rifle, and sometimes pistols."

In the 1840s several enterprising cattlemen gathered and drove herds east to Galveston or New Orleans where they shipped the cattle to market by sea. One rancher, Edward Piper, went northeast in 1846 and successfully piloted a herd of 1,000 steers all the way to Ohio. Other cattlemen drove herds to California after gold was discovered there in 1848. However, the hardships encountered during such long drives made the effort unprofitable for most ranchers.

When the Civil War began in 1861, the majority of men in Texas went east to fight for the Confederacy, and cattle raising came to an abrupt halt. When the war ended four years later, the Texans returned to find that cattle numbers in the state had increased to an estimated 3.5 million head. At the same time, the price per head had dropped from a high of $6 in 1860 to $3 in 1865, whereas in the northeastern United States a three year-old steer was worth in excess of $80.

Consequently, Texas cattlemen determined to locate markets in the northeast for their cattle and to drive them there. It was too late in 1865 for a cattle drive, so that winter they concentrated their efforts on gathering herds in preparation for driving north in the spring when grass would be sufficient to sustain their herds along the trail.

In 1866, Texas cattlemen sent an estimated 260,000 head north, mostly to the slaughter houses in St. Louis. Unfortunately, the drovers encountered numerous difficulties on the trail, primarily due to their own inexperience in making long cattle drives and their unfamiliarity with the country. Their problems were made worse by having to travel through rough and wooded terrain.

The main trail went west of Fort Worth and crossed the Red River into Indian Territory, populated by the Chickasaw, Choctaw, Creek, Cherokee, and Seminole Indians who were known as the Five Civilized Tribes. Many of these tribesmen demanded payment of steers in return for allowing the Longhorns to be driven across their land.

Once the herds reached the Missouri border, settlers attempted to stop the drives to protect their own stock from the tick fever that Texas cattle carried. Whereas Texas cattle were immune to the disease, large numbers of northern cattle became infected and died. As a result, many Missouri settlers armed themselves and successfully turned back most of the Texas herds.

Because of the difficulties encountered in their attempts to drive cattle to St. Louis, few Texas cattlemen reached a profitable destination with their herds in 1866. The exceptions were Oliver Loving and Charles Goodnight who, instead of going north, pioneered a cattle trail west from North Texas to the Horsehead Crossing of the Pecos River. The trail then followed the river into New Mexico to the Bosque Redondo Reservation where cattle were sold to feed the Navajo and Mescalero Apache Indians.

Later the trail was extended north to Las Vegas, New Mexico, where it then followed the Santa Fe Trail to Lucien Maxwell's ranch on the Cimarron River. From there it proceeded over Raton Pass and on to Denver, where the cattle were sold to feed miners in the Colorado gold fields. Several enterprising men also began to stock the grasslands east of the Rockies with Texas cattle. In 1874 an estimated 110,000 head of cattle were driven over the Goodnight-Loving Trail, comprising one-quarter of the total volume driven over trails to the north.

Fortunately for Texas cattlemen looking to send cattle to northern markets, the Kansas Pacific Railroad began building across Kansas in 1867. That year Joseph G. McCoy, an enterprising cattle dealer from Illinois, recognized the opportunity to develop a shipping point on the railroad, making it easier for producers to get their stock to market. He chose the small settlement of Abilene, Kansas, as the site for a cattle depot. It was an ideal location because the surrounding area was unsettled and well supplied with grass and water. Importantly, it was far enough west of the agricultural settlements of eastern Kansas and western Missouri that Texas cattle could be driven there without interference.

McCoy negotiated a contract with the Kansas Pacific by which he gained favorable shipping rates for buyers and also a percentage of the freight charges for himself. He constructed shipping pens at Abilene that were capable of accommodating 3,000 head of cattle. He also built a hotel, barns, and livery stables, which were ready for the cattlemen by early summer.

Loading cattle at McCoy's stockyard in Abilene, Kansas, 1867.

In July he sent W.W. Sugg south from Abilene to intercept any Texas herds that were trailing north. Sugg acquainted the trail bosses with the new shipping facilities in Kansas. Unfortunately, he started so late in the season that he was only able to lure 35,000 head of Texas cattle to Abilene that first year.

The next year, however, cattlemen in Texas learned of McCoy's cattle depot and trailed more than twice the number of Longhorns that had been shipped from Abilene the year before. The following year the number driven north to the railroad increased to a phenomenal 350,000 head.

The Texas cattle that reached Abilene were primarily purchased by Midwestern buyers who sent them to the Corn Belt states of Illinois, Indiana, and Ohio for fattening. In addition, United States government contractors came to Abilene to buy cattle to feed Indians that had been recently confined to various reservations west of the Mississippi River. When sold to these contractors, the cattle continued on the trail to the designated reservations.

Indians had hunted buffalo horseback on the plains for several centuries, but in the late 1860s most of the tribes signed treaties with the US government which restricted them to large tracts of land in the Dakota and Indian Territories. In return, the government agreed to feed and clothe the tribesmen, because the herds of buffalo that they subsisted on were being slaughtered by American hunters. In 1871 there were 250,000 Indians living on reservations west of the Mississippi. As a result, large numbers of Texas cattle were driven past the railheads in Kansas and trailed to the reservations.

Early in the 1860s cattlemen were unsure if Texas Longhorns could survive the harsh winters on the northern range. But after cattle had wintered for several years on the Dakota reservations, they proved that they not only grew fat in the North, but they matured to even larger sizes than they did in Texas. With that knowledge, Texans began trailing herds to the immense grasslands of Montana, Wyoming, Colorado, western Kansas, and Nebraska. Soon the southern ranges were used primarily as breeding grounds, while the northern ranges were devoted to fattening and maturing the cattle before they were shipped to Chicago for slaughter.

Abilene lost its position as the chief shipping point for Texas cattle after the 1871 season. It was replaced by Dodge City, Kansas, which had been built on the Santa Fe Railroad further southwest. From that time on, Dodge City became the most important cattle shipping point and the most memorable Kansas cow town in American history.

Drovers used two trails to drive cattle from South Texas to the Kansas railheads. The Chisholm Trail was used to reach Abilene, and it ran directly north from San Antonio across the Indian Territory. After Dodge City was established in 1872, cattlemen blazed what became known as the Western Trail. It started west of San Antonio, crossed the Red River at Doan's Store, and went across the reservations of the Kiowa, Comanche, Cheyenne, and Arapahoe. Once it reached Dodge City it continued north to the Union Pacific Railroad at Ogallala, Nebraska. From there branches went to the Dakota reservations or to the ranches of Wyoming and Montana.

After several years of experience taking herds up the trail, cattlemen discovered that 2,500 head was the optimal number for long drives. This number usually required twelve drovers who needed four to six horses in their mount. A chuckwagon, pulled by four mules and driven by the cook, carried the cowboys' beds and other equipment along with the food supplies. A horse wrangler was hired to ride herd on the saddle horses, which were referred to by the Spanish word *remuda*.

A trail herd could travel between ten and fifteen miles a day, which translated to between 300 and 500 miles per month at a cost of roughly $500. A drive undertaken by the XIT Ranch in 1892 was typical. That

New Mexico cowboys, 1880s.

Trail crew having a meal at the chuckwagon.

summer the ranch's cowboys took three and a half months to drive 2,500 head of steers from the Texas Panhandle to Miles City, Montana. The cost to the ranch was $1,800, which excluded horses, wagon, and equipment. Wages accounted for $1,350 and food costs were $386.

Trail bosses, who were responsible for guiding the herd to its destination and taking care of the crew's welfare, normally received $125 a month in wages. Cowboys were paid between $25 and $40 a month, while the cook received $5 more. Each cowboy furnished his own saddle and bed, while the company or owner supplied the horses.

Driving Longhorns up the trail was not for the faint of heart or for men of poor constitution. The potential problems were numerous and included flooding rivers, stampedes, falls from horses, lightning, and attacks by hostile Indians. The crew often consisted of cowboys from a wide variety of backgrounds, including former slaves and those of Hispanic descent. All hands showed great courage and skill in seeing their charges to the end of the trail.

While the early years of the Texas cattle business had been devoted to gathering and driving free-range stock to northern markets, once the Plains Indians settled on reservations and the buffalo had vanished, cattlemen began stocking grasslands all across the Great Plains to raise cattle for eastern markets. Charles Goodnight was one of the first to do this. In the spring of 1876 he drove cattle from his pastures in Colorado back to the Texas Panhandle after the Kiowa and Comanche Indians had been moved to an Indian Territory reservation.

Goodnight chose the Palo Duro Canyon at the head of the Red River as the site for his ranch. Before his cattle could take to this range, however, his cowboys had to drive herds of buffalo out of the area. From this new ranch, Goodnight's cowboys drove his steers to the railhead at Dodge City, Kansas.

By the late 1870s Texas cattlemen determined that the most efficient and cost-effective method of raising cattle was through large-scale operations. A few small ranchers successfully expanded their operations, but the majority eventually sold to the larger operators. The potential profits were great because the expenses were minimal for grazing cattle on public lands, while the selling price of cattle was at an all-time high. As a result, ranching in the West drew the interest of investors from the eastern United States and Great Britain, many of whom formed corporations to operate on a large scale.

Foreign investment was especially heavy. It was estimated that by 1885 foreigners controlled more than 20 million acres of public grazing lands in the West. The Prairie Cattle Company was a typical example. Formed by a Scottish syndicate, the company grazed more than 150,000 head of cattle in Texas, New Mexico, and Colorado.

The Matador Land and Cattle Company was another Scottish corporation and the only foreign-owned cattle company with a lifetime that extended into the twentieth century. Founded in 1882 and capitalized at more than $2.5 million, the company initially purchased more than 375,000 acres in West Texas and stocked the range with 75,000 head of cattle. By 1891 the Matador had increased its holdings to more than 5.5 million acres, as well as holding an additional 200,000 acres

XIT cowboys on the range.

in state leases. Murdo Mackenzie managed the Matador's far-flung operation that extended from Texas to Montana.

The Capitol Freehold Ranch or XIT was an example of an American syndicate organized to raise cattle. In 1879 the company accepted more than three million acres appropriated by the Texas Legislature, and the land lay in parts of nine counties of the west-ern Texas Panhandle. Eventually the XIT ran 160,000 head of cattle and branded more than 35,000 calves each spring.

The company fenced the entire ranch with barbed wire, dug 300 water wells, and instituted modern management techniques, including cross-fencing to create convenient-sized pastures.

In the early 1880s most of the large outfits tended to stock the range as fully as possible to take advantage of high cattle prices. Few of them owned the land where their cattle grazed, instead purchasing deeds to strategic water sources. By controlling access to water, they were able to control the surrounding range land.

1884 marked the peak for returns in the western cattle business. Cattlemen and cattle investors rode this high until it came crashing down as a result of an extremely harsh winter in 1886-1887. During that winter deep snows were followed by heavy winds and intense cold. Most cattle on the range were unable to get to grass. Those who could not find cover drifted aimlessly in the face of bitter winds. Thousands were trapped in ravines or canyons where they perished, while count-less others froze or died on the range from lack of water and feed.

The extent of the loss is illustrated by figures from Montana. In that state, more than 650,000 head of cattle had been assessed for taxes in 1886. After the hard winter the number assessed dropped by 200,000 head. Many eastern and foreign investors were forced out of business and sold what remained of their herds. With the market flooded, the price of cattle dropped drastically, reverberating throughout the entire industry.

The cattle raisers that survived subsequently reduced their herds and began purchasing European breeds, such as Durhams, Herefords, and

Angus, to cross with their Longhorn cows. The resulting "get" matured sooner and at a higher weight. Ranchers also began raising hay in the summer to supplement winter grass as feed for their herds.

Cattlemen began to purchase and fence the range that they used in order to better care for their improved stock. Barbed wire was invented by Joseph E. Glidden, who introduced it to Texas in 1875. Initially, many ranchers were slow to adopt it, believing that the barbs would injure their cattle. Once convinced of its effectiveness, however, they began using it widely. Some went so far as enclosing parts of the public domain until it became illegal in Texas in 1884. Fenced ranges required less labor and reduced cattle losses from straying and theft. In addition, cattlemen were better able to conserve the grassland and keep track of their stock.

Cattle ranching in the West was responsible for making beef a staple item in the American diet. Cattlemen and their cowboys were in the vanguard of settlement on the Great Plains, although their prominence was short-lived because wheat farmers soon followed and gained control of much of the public domain. Nonetheless, cattle ranching continued to thrive, and it remains an integral part of the western economy today. Cowboys still take care of cattle horseback, just as the first Indian *vaqueros* did several centuries ago.

Lead Steers

"I expect Charlie Goodnight and myself are 'bout the only trail bosses willing to admit that they can learn something from a good lead steer." —Colonel Jack *"Lead Steer"* Potter

Reading through the journals and reminiscences left by drovers who trailed cattle north out of Texas in the 1870s and '80s, one finds many references to the unsung heroes of the drives—the lead steers that guided herds to railheads in Kansas or to the northern ranges of Wyoming, Montana, and the Dakotas. From the accounts, a general picture emerges of the steers who, as self-appointed leaders, were instrumental in bringing the cattle drives through.

Among the cattle in each herd, there were several steers who were larger, stronger, faster, and more intelligent than the rest. By their very nature, these steers seemed to consider themselves superior to their brethren, so much so that sometimes they would not bed down with the rest of the herd. Lead steers were often among the wildest cattle in the herds. Although they could be approached on horseback, it was unthinkable for anyone to attempt to get near them on foot.

Each morning they took their place at the head of the drive. Even when their feet became tender and they were forced to drop to the rear, they resumed the lead once they came upon soft or sandy ground. From that position, the point men on each side could direct their movements, with the rest of the herd following behind.

They displayed their true value when it came time to cross a fast-running river. Because cattle are reluctant to take to high water, river crossings were accomplished more successfully when the herd was led by one of their own kind, rather than being pushed from behind or led by a man on horseback. Lead steers could be counted on to readily take their charges to the other side.

Some leaders, however, were not always enthusiastic about carrying out their responsibilities. An account of a drive in 1882 told of a herd that stalled on the Red River because of high water. The trail boss roped one of the leaders and, half dragging him, half leading him, took him into the river. This was enough to inspire the rest of the herd to make the crossing.

Perhaps the most famous of all lead steers was Charles Goodnight's *Old Blue*. Born about 1870 in the Nueces River country of Texas, *Blue* went with a herd as a three year-old over the Goodnight-Loving Trail to John Chisum's ranch on the Pecos River in New Mexico. In the fall of the following year he was found by Chisum's cowboys with an Apache arrow in his rump. They roped him, extracted the arrowhead, and turned him back onto the range.

Charles Goodnight unknowingly bought the steer in the spring of 1874 when he purchased 5,000 steers from Chisum. *Blue* went with part of the herd that was trailed north to Goodnight's ranch on the Arkansas River near Pueblo, Colorado. Range historian J. Frank Dobie wrote:

> From the day the herd trailed out, the steer asserted his natural leadership. Every morning he took his place at the point and there he held it. Powerful, sober, and steady, he understood the least motion of the point men, and in guiding the herd, showed himself worth a dozen extra hands.

Two years later when Goodnight decided to locate on Palo Duro Creek in the Texas Panhandle, *Blue* was in the lead of the 1,600 head of cattle destined for the stock range. Beginning in 1878, *Blue* led Goodnight beef herds to the railroad in Dodge City for eight consecutive years, sometimes making the trip twice in a single year. On each trip the cowboys strapped a bell around his neck, and the other steers followed the clanging bell. *Blue* was roped at night, and the clapper was muffled so the steer would not inadvertently disturb the herd.

The big steer was usually gentle and sociable. He often walked into camp at night in search of handouts from the cook, and he was frequently hobbled and turned out to graze with the saddle horses each evening.

A Texas longhorn steer.

He exhibited other qualities that were beyond normal bovine behavior. During stampedes he was known to step aside from the melee, stand his ground, and start bawling. The cowboys found that by doing this he helped to restore order to the herd. After the cattle had milled, they returned to their leader, beckoned by his call.

When *Blue* was no longer needed to lead the drives, Goodnight showed his gratitude by pensioning him out and letting him roam at will on the ranch. The steer died at age 20, and his horns were hung in a place of honor at the JA headquarters office.

Trail drover Bill Blocker's most memorable lead steer, a bay named *Pardner*, was not as fortunate as *Blue*. After leading a big herd to Abilene, Kansas, in 1870 the steer was sold with the rest of the bunch, even though at one point during the drive he was credited with saving Blocker's life.

While crossing the Salt Fork of the Arkansas River, the herd began to mill and Blocker lost his horse trying to break it up. As the drover floundered in the water, *Pardner* broke from the mill and swam past Blocker headed for the north bank. Blocker grabbed the steer's tail and was pulled safely across while the herd followed.

On a drive from Texas to Wyoming in 1877, Blocker's brother Ab had a work ox named *Bully* who became so fond of the outfit's chuck-wagon that he followed it everywhere when not in yoke. When the drive stalled at the icy and swollen Platte River, a bridge was located nearby and the wagon was driven across with *Bully* following close

behind. *Bully's* example caused the leaders to take the bridge, and soon the entire herd went across.

Perhaps no trail boss was as devoted to his lead steers as Jack Potter. Consequently he was given the sobriquet "Lead Steer." Jack named one of his favorite steers *Bob Wright* after a good friend who owned the largest mercantile in Dodge City. When Bob Wright the man saw *Bob Wright* the steer leading a herd across the swollen Arkansas River in the spring of 1884, he was so impressed that he said to Potter, "He is some lead steer all right. When you get back to Dodge this fall, call around. I'm going to make you a present of a John B. Stetson."

Lew Wallace was another steer that Potter greatly admired. The big black steer had led a number of herds for different drovers before Potter became acquainted with him while camped on the New England Livestock Company range southwest of Fort Sumner, New Mexico, in the 1880s. The steer made a habit of meeting Potter in camp each day when the cowman rode in from his circle.

One drive that *Lew Wallace* led for Potter was to the railroad at Clayton, and it crossed a dry stretch of more than 80 miles. When the herd finally came to water, Potter slid from his horse into the river, but found his tongue was so swollen that he could not drink. After

Lew Wallace had filled up, he took notice of the trail boss and seemed to comprehend that something was wrong. He stuck out his tongue, which Potter took as a message. He started throwing water on his own tongue and was soon able to drink.

When the herd reached Clayton, Potter split it into several train-load-sized bunches and *Lew Wallace* successively led each bunch into the shipping pens. After the last train was loaded, Potter happened to walk by one of the cars and heard a distinctive, although sad and mournful, "Moo-oo." He immediately recognized it as *Lew Wallace*. After chastising himself for allowing the steer to be loaded, he asked the train engineer to back up the car so *Lew Wallace* could be put off.

At that point the cattle buyer walked up and told Potter he would not sell back the steer because he had seen how he led the herds into the shipping pens. The cattle were destined for the Sioux Indian reservation where the agent was having trouble penning range cattle for the Indians to butcher. *Lew Wallace* was the perfect solution. The buyer promised that the big steer would be sheltered, fed, and treated like a lead steer should be. Assured that the steer would die of old age, Potter reluctantly bid his old friend farewell.

Baylis John Fletcher, who went up the trail in 1879, recorded a rare instance when lead steers got an outfit into trouble. Fletcher reported that one day the big steers who "always led the herd saw a heap of earth and ran bellowing to it. They began to paw it with their forefeet and toss the turf with their horns."

The cowboys didn't realize that the cattle were destroying a homesteader's abode until "a woman came running out from an opening in the ground and [began] fighting the steers frantically with her sun bonnet." The riders came to her aid as soon as possible, only to find the roof of the dugout had already caved in.

The woman was so distraught over the destruction of her home that when the cowboys offered their "services to help rebuild it, she disdainfully declined them, declaring that persons who were so ignorant as to allow their cattle to destroy the dugout could do little toward repairing it." The cowboys regretfully drove the herd off without receiving her forgiveness.

Oh, your backs they are weak,
And your legs they ain't strong.
Don't be skeered little dogies,
We'll git there 'fore long.
From dawn until midnight
We strike down the trail,
Just ya foller yer leaders
And hold up yer tail.

—Traditional Trail Song

Buffalo Runners

Much has been written about the great benefits that resulted when American Indians acquired Spanish horses on the Great Plains in the late seventeenth century. Anthropologist James Mooney wrote in 1898,

> Without the horse the Indian was a half-starved skulker in the timber, creeping up on foot towards the unwary deer or building a brush corral with infinite labor to surround a herd of antelope, and seldom venturing more than a few days' journey from home. With the horse he was transformed into the daring buffalo hunter, able to procure in a single day enough food to supply his family for a year, leaving him free to sweep the plains with his war parties along a range of a thousand miles.

Prior to acquiring horses, Indians hunted buffalo by either surrounding small herds on foot, impounding them in log and brush enclosures, or running them over cliffs. Each of these methods often resulted in the death of more animals than the natives could use. Mounted horseback, however, a hunter could selectively kill the number, age, and sex of the buffalo that he desired. As a result, most scholars agree that Indians on the Plains killed fewer buffalo annually after they acquired horses than before.

Buffalo (*bison bison*) were an unequaled source of the essentials for life. Along with consuming every edible part of the animal, Indians used the hides for teepee covers, robes, shields, moccasin soles, sinews for bowstrings, ribs for knives, hooves for glue, horns for spoons, and paunches for cooking.

The fact that horses also served as beasts of burden allowed the Indians of the Great Plains to substantially increase the volume and variety of their material possessions. They were able to make larger teepees than when they only used dogs to transport their lodges. At the same time, larger family groups were able to live together because of the more substantial and reliable food supply that their buffalo hunts provided. As a result, the social and political organization of the tribes began to develop in complexity.

Once the Kiowa, Comanche, Sioux, Cheyenne, Arapaho, Crow, and Blackfoot tribes acquired horses, they became constantly mobile as they wandered the prairies in search of fresh grass for their large herds. In fact, finding forage for their horses was a greater concern for them than locating buffalo to hunt. Consequently, they have often been described by anthropologists as horse pastoralists. The great numbers of horses they accumulated forced them to spread out in smaller family units during the winter when forage was scarce. When the grass came up in the spring, they would again join together in larger groups. During midsummer each tribe generally conducted a communal buffalo hunt after their most important annual ritual, the Sun Dance.

Given that horses were so valuable to their culture, an important focus of Plains Indian life was the on-going attempt to augment their herds through raids on Indian, Spanish, or Anglo enemies. Stolen horses had the additional value of already being broken to ride. An elaborate system of inter-tribal wars developed around horse stealing, and it became the way in which men gained rank and prestige within a tribe. The number of horses a warrior owned was also the gauge with which his wealth was determined in the tribe.

Horses were also acquired through trade with others and by capturing wild horses that roamed the prairies. In addition, most Plains Indians selectively bred the better mares from their herds in hopes of developing better mounts for raiding and hunting. Gentling domesticated colts inevitably proved to be more efficient than attempting to tame wild ones.

Horses used to hunt buffalo were by far the most prized among those owned by Plains Indians, and many Indians would not part with their favorite buffalo runner at any price. The major reason buffalo runners were highly valued was because they had a rare and special temperament. Horses and buffalo have a natural aversion to one another, and it took an animal of exceptional courage, endurance, and agility to willingly run beside a stampeding buffalo in order for a hunter to accurately shoot an arrow from a bow into its vitals. Buffalo runners were most often kept as stallions because ungelded horses were considered stronger and capable of pursuing their quarry longer.

Since the attributes required for a hunting horse and a war horse were similar, many Plains Indians used the same cherished mount for both purposes. Warriors often staked these favored animals near their

lodges at night, not only to protect them against raiders, but so that the owners could easily lavish them with affection as well.

The method of hunting buffalo on horseback followed a fairly common pattern among all tribes, including the Plains farming peoples such as the Pawnee, Osage, Mandan, Arikara, and Hidatsa. Primary hunts were conducted cooperatively during the summer when the buffalo were fat and the horses were in shape for running. Additional hunts were carried out in November and December when the hides were best for winter robes.

Once a large herd of buffalo was located, the village was alerted and preparations were begun that included dances to beseech the Great Spirit to ensure the success of the hunt and to make their ponies run swiftly. Usually a temporary hunting camp was established near the herd after the hunters had prepared their weapons and made medicine over their horses.

Members of the tribe's military societies, the "dog soldiers," directed the movement of the hunt to ensure that it was carried out in an orderly fashion. The soldiers were responsible for placing the hunters in position and giving them the command to begin. If a hunter started before the soldiers' signal, his horse was shot as a consequence.

The hunters rode bareback and usually wore nothing more than a breechclout. One eyewitness to a hunt in 1820 wrote that "once in

sight of the herd, the hunters gave kindly advice to their horses not to fear the bison, to run well, and not be gored." Once the hunt commenced, buffalo runners rarely required any physical encouragement from their riders. They willingly went to the buffalo after the hunter made his intention known.

Guiding their horses by knee pressure, the hunters approached their targets on the right side and aimed their weapons at the soft spot between the protruding hip bone and the last rib. Often an arrow was shot with such force that it became completely buried inside or went entirely through the buffalo. Sometimes the hunter was able retrieve an arrow from the side of a running victim and use it again. Each hunter marked his arrows so that he could claim the results of his hunt once he had shot all the arrows in his quiver.

Some hunters chose to hunt with a lance, which required special skill and nerve. In this way a warrior hunted until his horse became winded. Interestingly, some hunters were known to ride close enough to a buffalo to jump on its back and then kill it with a knife.

The buffalo-running horse was trained to swerve away upon hearing the twang of the bowstring in order to avoid being gored when the injured animal turned and charged. Unfortunately, some were not quick enough and had to be left by their masters on the hunting grounds.

Even after the Plains Indians acquired guns in the mid-nineteenth century they continued to use bows and arrows and lances to hunt buffalo. By that time the old flint points had been replaced with metal ones. The first single-shot muzzleloading muskets that the Plains Indians used were of little value horseback because of the difficulty in reloading them. Later, however, after they acquired repeating rifles and revolvers, they used them during their hunts. Nevertheless, most Plains Indian hunters continued to use their traditional weapons until there were no longer any buffalo to hunt as a result of the mass slaughter by white hunters in the 1870s and 1880s.

The apex of Plains Indian culture occurred within a relatively short time, based on buffalo hunting using horses. Nonetheless, it provides a sterling historical example of how horses, through their courage and loyalty, have aided humans in making a better life.

The First Roundup

On a clear day in September 1599, sixty Spanish soldiers rode forth from their headquarters on the Rio Grande. The sun glistened off their armor as they crossed the river and headed east, destined for the high plains of the Llano Estacado. Don Juan de Oñate, the leader of the newly established Spanish colony in New Mexico, had ordered the expedition to find buffalo. After locating the "native cattle," as the Spaniards referred to them, the soldiers were to gather a herd and drive it back to the colony. Oñate hoped that a breeding herd of the wild animals could be established to serve as food for the settlers.

The Spaniards only knew about buffalo from information supplied by the local Indians, and up to that time most of them had never actually seen a buffalo. But from what they had learned, they were satisfied that the wild animals could be handled much like their own domestic cattle. After spending a short time on the plains, however, they quickly understood that buffalo were much wilder than any bovine they had ever seen.

The expedition, under the command of Sergeant Major Vincente de Zaldivar, was well equipped with supplies and "many droves of mares" for packing and riding. The soldiers first traveled east to the Pecos

Sketch of a buffalo drawn by a member of the Oñate expedition.

Early drawing of a vast buffalo herd spread across the plains as far as the eye can see.

River and then proceeded to the foot of the mountains where they met a group of Indians who furnished them with a guide to find the buffalo.

After a few more days of traveling across the plains of eastern New Mexico, the expedition climbed on top of the caprock and for the first time saw buffalo watering at a playa lake. The next day they came upon a herd estimated at a thousand head. Zaldivar decided to build a large corral to pen as many as possible. Unfortunately the herd moved to the east before the soldiers finished the corral, so they abandoned it and followed the tracks of the herd.

In a few days the soldiers reached a spot south of the Canadian River where they discovered evidence of a large herd that had recently been driven off by Indians. A day later the Spaniards encountered another group of Indians and decided to camp near them. During the next few days, Zaldivar made several observations about how the Indians lived.

He was notably impressed by the serviceability of their tents "made of tanned hides, very bright red and white in color and bell-shaped, with flaps and openings, and built as skillfully as those of Italy." He further noted that "the tanning is so fine that, although it should rain bucketfuls, it will not pass through nor stiffen the hide, but rather upon drying it remains as soft and pliable as before." Even though the tents were large, able to accommodate "four different mattresses," he commented that they did not weigh more than fifty pounds.

Zaldivar was amused at how the natives transported their belongings using "medium-sized shaggy dogs" as pack animals. The Indians had great numbers of them. In his account of the expedition he reported that "it is a sight worth seeing and very laughable to see them traveling...nearly all of them snarling in their encounters, traveling one after another on their journey. In order to load them, the Indian women seize their heads between their knees, and thus load them or adjust the load, which is seldom required because they travel along at a steady gait as if they had been trained by means of reins."

The Spaniards continued their march after a few days, and soon found another large buffalo herd. Several members of the expedition estimated that it contained more cattle than could be found on "three of the largest ranches in new Spain." As a result, Zaldivar again ordered his men to build a corral, which they completed in three days. It was constructed of cottonwood logs, and was so large that the Spaniards believed it would hold 10,000 head.

When the corral was finished, the soldiers made plans to pen the buffalo. They were still under the assumption that the animals would be easy to pen, primarily because they seemed nearly tame, given how closely they wandered past the camp. Furthermore, the Spaniards were convinced that buffalo were poor runners because of their ungainly appearance. However, in the next several days they would learn firsthand how intractable those "native cattle" could be.

The Spaniards' first attempt at driving buffalo started out well enough, although it soon went awry. The soldiers got behind a big bunch and slowly headed them toward the wings of the corral. But as the buffalo neared the wings, the leaders of the herd turned back and stampeded toward the surprised soldiers. The expedition's chronicler, Juan Bocanegra, described the occasion by saying, "It was impossible to stop them because they are terribly obstinate cattle, courageous beyond exaggeration, and so cunning that if pursued they run, and if their pursuers stop or slacken their speed, they stop and roll, just like mules, and with this respite renew their run."

In the following days the Spaniards made several more attempts to pen the buffalo, but all were equally

Spanish soldier horseback on the Great Plains.

unsuccessful. They discovered to their dismay that buffalo were not as docile as they first appeared. Bocanegra described them as being "remarkably savage and ferocious, so much so that they killed three of our horses and badly wounded forty" others. He wrote that the buffalo attack from the side with their sharp horns "so that whatever they seize they tear very badly."

Having failed at driving the buffalo into the corral, Zaldivar decided on a new strategy. He ordered his men to bring in calves because he recognized the futility of trying to rope adults. Unfortunately, even though his soldiers caught many calves, none of them survived the stress of being drug or even carried on a horse.

Thoroughly frustrated, Zaldivar finally turned the expedition back to the Rio Grande and reported to Oñate the results of his unsuccessful mission. From his experience on the plains, he suggested that the only way buffalo could ever be driven to the colony would be to crossbreed them with Spanish bulls in hopes that the calves could be gentled enough to drive. Unfortunately, history provides no record that this experiment was ever carried out.

Lore of the Leather Throne

Whether a cowpuncher rode a double-cinch rig or a buckaroo sat a single-cinch saddle, cowboys developed a large body of lore relating to their most important tool—the stock saddle. This lore, laced with colorful expressions, allowed them to convey complex thoughts with few words. Many of these historical idioms, collected by Texan Ramon F. Adams, are still in use throughout cattle country today.

Cowboy artist Charles Russell cogently described the two basic saddle traditions of the West in "The Story of the Cowpuncher." He wrote that "Texas an' California, bein' the startin' places, made two species of cowpunchers. Those west of the Rockies...used centerfire or single-cinch saddles with high forks an' cantle," whereas "the cowpuncher east of the Rockies...rode a saddle [that had] a low horn [and was a] rimfire or double-cinch."

The terms centerfire and rimfire were comparisons to spent rifle cartridges. After being fired, a centerfire cartridge shows one mark in the brass casing's center where the firing pin hit the cartridge. The rimfire cartridge used in Model 1866 Winchester rifles displayed two marks on opposite sides of the rim, made when the forked firing pin struck the cartridge. Centerfire saddles were also referred to as being single-rigged or single-barreled

or as California rigs. Rimfire saddles were said to be either double-rigged, double-fired, or double-barreled.

Throughout the West a saddle was spoken of in general terms as a cow saddle, a range saddle, or most commonly as a stock saddle. When using slang, a cowboy might call his saddle a "wood" or "tree," which referred to the wooden tree upon which the leather housing was built. In addition, a saddle might be called a "kack," "leather," "hull" or "*montura*," from its Spanish name.

The song "The Old Chisholm Trail" begins, "On a $10 hoss and a $40 saddle." This refers to a time long past when, because of the abundance of horses, their cost was a fraction of the amount spent on the saddle they carried. Generally, a man's saddle was his most expensive piece of equipment, often costing the equivalent of one or two months' wages. That generally holds true even today.

As an indication of the importance of a man's saddle to him, in a poker game a cowboy might wager his spurs, his gun, or even his boots, but never his saddle. In other words, a man couldn't be a cowboy if he didn't own a saddle. Because a man made his living with his saddle, he took great pride in it. It was the item in his outfit that he took the best care of. He kept it off the ground whenever he could, greased it often, and frequently checked the condition of the latigos, cinches, and strings.

A cowpuncher disliked having to borrow a saddle, just as much as he hated to loan a saddle to someone. Phillip Ashton Rollins explained in his book *The Cowboy, An Unconventional History of Civilization on the Old-Time Cattle Range* that "each saddle gradually acquired tiny humps and hollows that registered with [a cowboy's] anatomy and induced both comfort and security of seat." Consequently, one man's saddle was rarely comfortable for someone else. Rollins related a story about one cowboy telling another, "Don't bother to get your saddle, ride mine. It's the best that ever came out of Cheyenne." The man accepted, but on returning from his ride asked his friend, "Where in the hell did you ever find this Spanish Inquisition chamber?"

When a man saddled, he was said to "slap his tree on," "put his leather on," or "stick his kack on" the horse. A cowboy never carried his saddle to the horse he was going to ride—he brought the horse to the saddle. Also, he always saddled and unsaddled his own horse, and any offer of help was unwelcome unless he was physically unable to do it himself.

When a man was told to "put his saddle in the wagon," it signified that he was fired and was obligated to leave the ranch. A rider was judged to be experienced, wise, dependable, and trustworthy when other complimented him by saying he was "settin' deep in his tree."

When a cowhand retired or became too old to ride, it was said that he'd "hung up his saddle" or "hung his saddle on the fence." Further, when a man "sacked his saddle" it meant he'd passed away. This saying relates to trail drive days when a man put his saddle in a sack after a drive in order to transport it on the train for the return home. This figure of speech conveyed that the cowboy was on the journey to his eternal home.

Perhaps the worst thing a cowboy could do was to sell his saddle. That desperate act implied he was giving up the occupation which his kind thought superior to all others. Metaphorically, when a man "sold his saddle" it meant that he was either broke or had fallen into disgrace by betraying the trust of his friends.

Rollins related an old range country story about the ranch kid who, after reading his American history book and learning about Benedict Arnold, was asked by his teacher to comment on the traitor's actions. The young boy thought hard for a minute and then replied, "He was one of our generals, and he sold his saddle."

Whenever a man got thrown and looked up to see his horse running away with his saddle, he would often cry out to his partners, "Ketch my saddle!" The horse was not his primary concern because it belonged to the company. The saddle, however, was not only his possession, but his most prized one as well. As for riding broncs, there's a range adage that says, "A

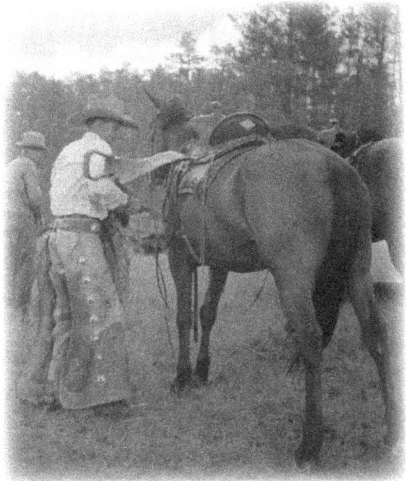

saddle seat's the easiest thing to find, but the hardest to keep." That's why inexperienced riders have always been encouraged to "ride the horse, not the saddle."

There's another popular range story about a cowpuncher who, while riding a pitching horse, lost a stirrup. At the same time the bronc caught a hind foot in that same stirrup, and the cowboy hit the ground. When asked what happened, he replied, "When I looked down and saw that bronc's foot in the stirrup I said to myself, 'If he's gettin' on, then I'm gettin' off.'"

When one man attempted to bluff, blame, or "ride" another, the cowboys remarked that he was trying to "put the saddle on him." Whereas when a man was said to "saddle a dead horse" on another, it meant that he was "saddling" him with an unwanted obligation.

During the trot back to headquarters at the end of a long day, one cowboy might say of another that he was "savin' saddle leather," which meant that he was standing in his stirrups in order to stretch, and his seat didn't touch the seat of the saddle. Tenderfeet were notorious for doing the same thing, although not for the same reason. They simply were trying to ease their saddle sores.

"Good saddles don't
make good riders."

—Will James

What Happened to Quirts?

In his 1946 book *Trail Dust and Saddle Leather*, Jo Mora wrote, "There was a time when the cowpuncher and his quirt were about as inseparable as the cowpuncher and his spurs...You'll seldom see one in these days...It seems that the old-time quirt is slowly wiggling its way into the museum cabinet of past range history."

Mora was right. One would be hard pressed to find a quirt among a modern horsebreaker's equipment as he corrals a bunch of colts for their first saddles. Equally as difficult would be to find a ranch cowboy today carrying one on his saddle while gathering cattle during the spring or fall works.

The old-time quirt was a short flexible whip plaited of rawhide or leather. It averaged 30 to 36 inches in total length. Its name was derived from the Spanish *cuarta de cordon*, meaning whip of cord. Quirts were made in many designs. Some had stiff handles with wood or rawhide cores, while others were made with handles loaded with lead shot to give them weight. A leather or rawhide strap was added to one end of the handle for carrying. Two leather lashes or "poppers" were attached to the other end.

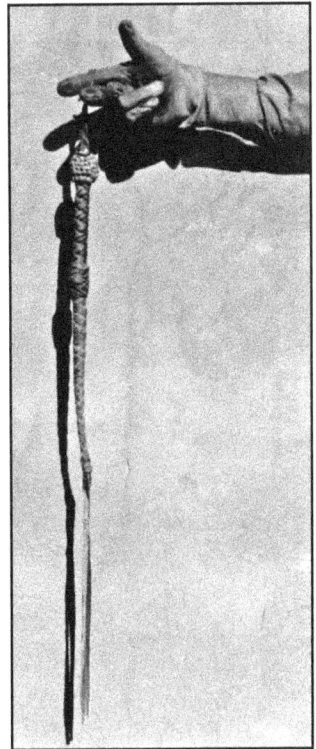

Mora rode the length of the southwestern cow country during the first decades of the 1900s. Although an astute observer of the cowboys he rode with and their methods for handling cows and horses, he was unable to explain why quirts later disappeared from cowboy saddles. He firmly believed them to be valuable and necessary tools, not only in the early handling of broncs, but in their later education in neck reining and cow work as well. He was evidently unaware of the dramatic changes in saddle stock and handling methods that had come about since his active days in the saddle.

In the days Mora described, a quirt was an essential item in every horsebreaker's outfit. Generally a raw bronc was roped in the corral, saddled, and immediately mounted. Sometimes the bronc-twister might take time to tie up a hind foot and sack out a bronc before climbing on. Once mounted, however, he invariably used a quirt on either the bronc's nose, shoulder, or hind leg to whip "the buck" out of him if he offered.

Many horsebreakers used a quirt with a lash made from a two-inch doubled stub of latigo (off billet). The loud popping of this type of quirt essentially scared the bronc into submission. It was popular because it would not leave welts on the bronc's hide. The technique was effective if the rider could sit the bronc well enough to use the quirt each time the horse made a jump, thus making him afraid to buck because of the retribution he would receive. Actually, using the quirt helped the rider better keep in rhythm with the bronc's motions. Once a bronc was allowed to buck without quirting, however, he often pitched each time a rider stepped on, whether quirted or not.

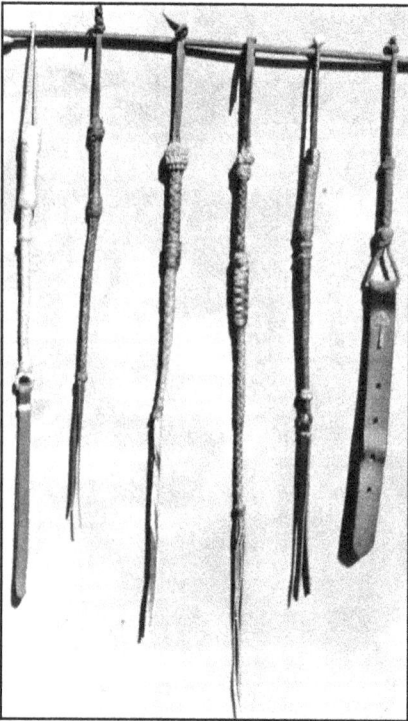

The lash of the quirt was believed to be more effective than spurs in persuading a horse not to buck. There was an old saying in cow country that "spurs put the buck in a horse, and a quirt took it out." Many horsebreakers chose not to wear spurs (and still don't) when starting colts. Some ranchers even made it company policy that spurs weren't to be used on young horses. The fear was that an inadvertent jab with a spur at the wrong time might provoke a colt or at least distract him from his lessons.

In those days ranch horses were mostly of cold-blooded Mustang or half-bred stock—Mustang mares crossed with pure-bred stallions. They were usually broken when they were between four and six years old. The big outfits need-

Sketch by Frank Hoffman.

ed large numbers of replacement horses in short periods of time to keep their cowboys sufficiently mounted. A cattleman couldn't allow his horsebreaker several days gentling a bronc on the ground before the first ride. Most broncs bucked out of fear, and it was the twister's job to whip it out of them. The process was often extremely hard on both horse and rider.

During the 1920s and '30s, many cattlemen began upgrading their saddle stock using Thoroughbred blood, the precursors of the modern Quarter Horse. The resultant get was higher strung and didn't take as well to rough handling as did the old type broncs. In addition, they were started earlier as two and three year-olds when they would gentle down faster. Many of these better bred colts never offered to buck, while others bucked only half-heartedly and were easily persuaded from it.

The same period saw many of the old-time outfits divided into ranches which required fewer horses to carry out their cow work. With the increased cost of raising higher quality colts, many ranchers realized the necessity of investing more time in the initial breaking and training of colts. They recognized that a greater percentage of their well-bred colts would turn out better than the Mustang-type colts. As a result, horsebreakers resorted to their quirts less often.

Nonetheless, quirts didn't quite disappear. Although most horsebreakers and cowboys no longer found them necessary to punish broncs when they bucked, they continued to use them in teaching started colts to neck rein and spin. A tap with a quirt on either shoulder, in connection with an opposite pull of the rein, sped up a colt's neck reining education. When used judiciously, a colt learned to respect and respond to the quirt, rather than fearing it.

Jo Mora wrote that almost every cowboy and horsebreaker had a quirt as part of his outfit. A cowpuncher was not always fortunate enough to have calm, well-broke horses with a lightning neck rein. In any man's string of horses it was possible to find mounts that had developed bad habits at some point, such as bucking, rearing, or simply being lazy. A quirt came in handy with such horses.

When a horse or bronc threatened to turn over backward, a cowboy could strike him between the ears with the quirt handle to get him to return to all fours. Unfortunately, some horses were injured or even killed as a result, but the action undoubtedly saved a number of cowpunchers from starting their own premature journey across the Great Divide.

A lazy or tired horse could be prompted to look alive with the lash of a quirt. Old-time quirt-carrying cowboys have said that they could get more out of a tired horse with a quirt than they could with spurs. It was important for the rider to continually swing the quirt in view of the horse. That way the horse was not so apt to be surprised or frightened when it was necessary to apply the lash.

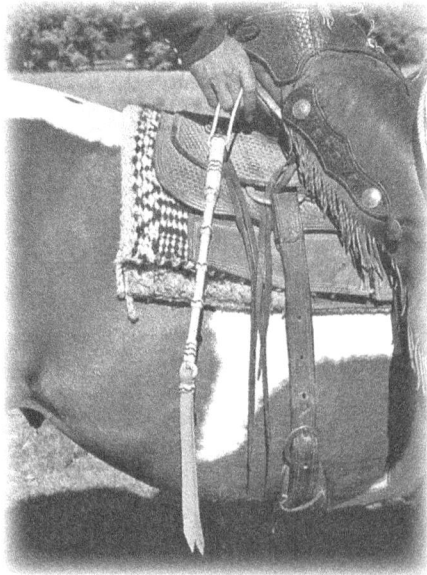

While horseback, a cowboy could carry a quirt on his wrist or hang it from his saddle horn. Many quirts were equipped with a small metal ring plaited into the handle that could be attached to a snap on one of the rear jockey saddle strings. Carried in this manner, the quirt was out of the way when the cowboy had to pull down his lariat.

Through the years, the western cattle industry has experienced change in almost every phase of operation due to technological and breeding advanc-

es. Modern cow and horse behavior is often dramatically different from that found in western cows and horses before the turn of the twentieth century. Methods and equipment employed to handle cows and horses have been adapted accordingly, becoming more sophisticated and refined. Other methods and equipment have become obsolete because of changing conditions.

The use of the quirt is a telling example. With modern horsebreakers spending more time gentling their broncs at an earlier age, they no longer need to resort to heavy-handed techniques. This is not to say that quirts couldn't be used in breaking, training, and disciplining modern horses. The practical techniques of using them effectively have been lost simply due to the absence of a need to pass on that knowledge to subsequent generations. If quirts have found their way into the museum cabinet, it is because there is no need to use them on the range where they were once so numerous.

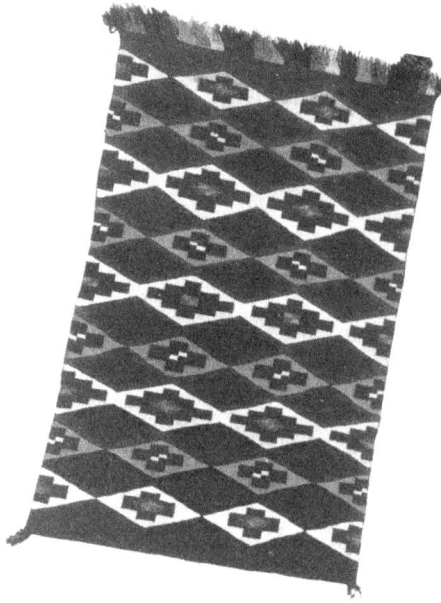

Navajo Saddle Blankets

Part of the enjoyment of looking at a Charles Russell painting comes in studying the details of the picture. Whether one focuses on the carving of a saddle, the knot of a cowpuncher's neckerchief, or the bead work on a Blackfoot woman's dress, Russell's paintings are valuable documents that can be used to determine how Montana cowboys and Indians of the latter part of the 19th century dressed and what kinds of horse equipment they used. In that regard it is interesting to note that Russell painted many of his cowpunchers using Navajo blankets as saddle pads, even though the source for those blankets was hundreds of miles south in New Mexico and Arizona.

Women of the Navajo tribe have woven blankets since the early 1700s when the tribe first acquired *churro* sheep from Spanish settlers along the northern Rio Grande. From the outset sheep were important to the Navajo economy, not only for wool, but as a source of meat as well. The Navajos learned how to shear, wash, and card wool and spin it into yarn from their neighbors, the Pueblo Indians, who also taught them how to color the yarn using native plant dyes.

Blankets were woven on upright looms constructed of juniper pole

A family of Navajo weavers. Notice the woman at the loom, the woman on the right fashioning a sash, and the young girl in the foreground carding wool.

frames that were easily taken apart and moved when migrating from place to place. For almost two centuries the primary weavings made by Navajo women were *serapes* or wearing blankets which averaged 4½ by 6 feet in size. These early blankets, which were woven in simple arrangements of stripes, were lightweight and so finely crafted that they would repel water. They were valuable trade items between the Navajos and the Pueblo tribes on the Rio Grande, who then traded them to the Kiowas, Comanches, and Cheyennes across the southern Plains. Some Navajo blankets were traded as far away as the Lakota tribes on the northern Plains.

Along with wearing blankets, the Navajos also wove strong and durable saddle blankets which were heavier and coarser in weave. These smaller blankets were woven with natural grey, brown, or black wool in horizontal stripes or twill and diamond twill weaves. Often the stripes were further embellished with zigzags, wavy lines, and diamonds in combinations of red, white, and indigo blue.

The Navajos were great horsemen. They relied on their horses not only to herd their sheep but to make raids against their enemies. Because they prized their horses, they were fond of decorating their horse equipment such as trimming their bridles with silver and turquoise and pounding brass nails into their Mexican saddles. The preferred way for a Navajo to finish off a horse outfit was to lay down one of his own brightly colored wool blankets under the saddle.

By the 1870s the Navajos were encouraged by white traders to make fewer wearing blankets because of the growing competition with American textile manufacturers who mass produced wool blankets. These machine-made blankets were woven in brilliant colors and intricate geometric designs that were immediately popular with reservation Indians all over the West. They were only slightly less durable than handmade Navajo blankets, but they were much less expensive.

Instead of weaving wearing blankets, the traders urged the Navajos to weave floor rugs and saddle blankets for sale to white customers. They assisted the weavers by stocking commercial dyes in a wide range of colors including red, orange, and green so that they could more easily dye their yarn. They also carried commercially spun and dyed wool yarns that were ready for the weavers' use. Through these efforts, the weavers soon provided large quantities of smaller pieces that found a ready market throughout the West. The rugs were woven in various designs, and exact duplicates were rarely produced. Saddle blankets, on the other hand, continued to be woven in traditional patterns.

The earliest saddle blankets the Navajos made were roughly thirty inches square. The blankets made at the end of the nineteenth century, however, were woven twice that size so that they could be folded in half to provide more cushioning under the heavier, American-made

stock saddles the Navajos had begun riding. The blankets were woven in red, black, grey, white, orange, yellow, blue, and green, sometimes in stripes, but often in large diamonds or zigzag lines. Often the Navajo weavers would attach yarn tassels to the corners or ends of the blankets. Sometimes a weaver made half the blanket in one design and finished the other half in a different design, thereby giving the user a reversible saddle pad.

It was during this time that cowboys in the Southwest discovered the value and attractiveness of Navajo blankets as saddle pads and began to use them extensively. They discovered what the Navajos had long known, that the native-made blankets absorbed sweat well, could be washed, and lasted longer than most other horse blankets. Soon cowpunchers from Canada to Mexico were riding Navajo blankets under their saddles. At the turn of the century the famous Navajo trader Lorenzo Hubbell reported that he made a greater profit on the wholesale of saddle blankets than he did on rugs. His best sellers went from 75¢ to a dollar a pound.

By the 1930s saddle shops all over the West were carrying a wide selection of Navajo saddle blankets on their shelves and in their catalogs. The blankets were sold in the range of $1.25 to $2.50 a pound depending on the thickness and fineness of the weave. They sold blankets of different qualities, many of which could be used either as a saddle blanket or as a rug on the bunkhouse floor. Many cowboys bought Navajo blankets for use as winter covers on their beds. When the blan-

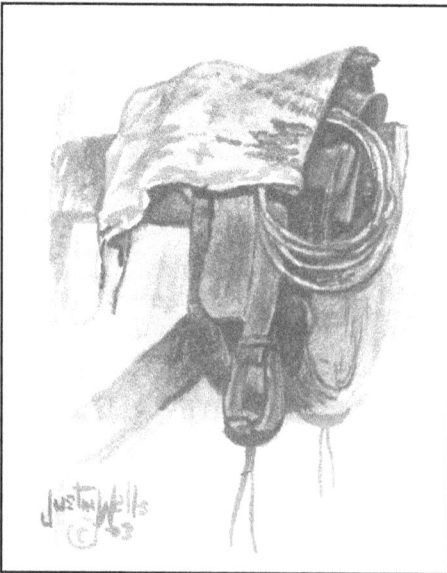

ket they were riding wore out, they had another one ready for use. They would then replace the bed covering at the next opportunity.

Navajo weavers still make good saddle blankets today. They are no longer sold by the pound but instead cost around $150 for singles or twice that for doubles. In keeping with Navajo tradition, today's blankets are thicker and a bit coarser in weave than floor rugs and wall hangings, but they are still made in twill or diamond twill weaves along with stripes and patterns of red, black, grey, and white. The craftsmanship remains superior.

Those who like the look of Navajo blankets, but consider the cost prohibitive, might consider blankets woven in Mexico that are readily available in many saddle shops. Mexican blankets are woven on mechanical treadle looms which enable the weavers to produce them more rapidly than Navajo weavers, thus decreasing the price. The blankets from south of the border are woven with both wool and wool blend yarns. A major difference in the two types of blankets is that the Mexican weavers use cotton warps (lengthwise yarns), while the Navajos use wool. Nevertheless, Mexican blankets wear well and can be easily washed like Navajo blankets.

Mexican saddle blankets are woven in assorted stripes, but use a wider range of colors. Many of them closely follow traditional Navajo rug and blanket patterns. However, they do not display the individual variation seen in Navajo blankets. No matter which is chosen, a rider can be certain of having a handsome blanket that will wear well, last a long time, and won't sore a horse.

Cowboy Wish-books

In his book, *Big Enough*, Will James described how the main character, Billy, learned to read and write from studying saddle catalogs with his mother at the family ranch. Whether in fact anyone ever learned the three R's from studying a catalog, James' story illustrates how important saddle manufacturers' catalogs have been in the life of the American cowboy.

From the time catalogs were first issued by saddle makers, they have ranked as one of the most popular forms of reading material on ranches throughout the West. Often referred to as "Cowboy Bibles," saddle catalogs were, and are, the working cowboy's wish book. Even if a man was not in need of a new saddle or pair of spurs, he still spent a good portion of his leisure time pouring over the pages of his favorite catalogs.

A bunkhouse could rarely be found without a stack of current and outdated catalogs located somewhere inside. As cowboys drifted to other ranges, they often left behind the catalogs they had accumulated so that their partners could thumb through them whenever they had a chance.

Lee Rice, who chronicled the history of many old saddle manufacturers in his book, *They Saddled the*

West, credits Frank Meanea with issuing the first illustrated saddlery catalog featuring his soon-to-be famous Cheyenne saddles in 1874. Other large manufacturers followed suit, including the Visalia Stock Saddle Company which produced a catalog in the mid-1880s, R.T. Frazier of Pueblo in 1890, Hamley's of Pendleton in 1909, and Porter's of Phoenix in 1910.

Catalogs were the primary means of advertisement for saddle manufacturers, and they often created a national reputation. Mail order sales from catalogs represented the bulk of retail sales for many manufacturers up to World War II or in the days when transportation was slower and the population in the West was more scattered than today. The T. Flynn Company of Pueblo is said to have recorded ninety per cent of its business as catalog sales before it closed its doors in 1926.

The evolution of fully illustrated saddle catalogs began with simple pressboard cards that had one or two photographs of saddles on one side and a current price list on the other. Next, several companies pioneered the use of pamphlets illustrated with representative examples of their saddles, chaps, headstalls, reins, quirts, harness, and other items.

By 1920 the "golden age" of saddlery catalogs had begun, and this period was to last until the early 1940s. During this time the larger manufacturers issued catalogs of well over one hundred pages which were filled with sophisticated pictorial layouts of not only saddles, but lines of goods calculated to satisfy every want or need a cowboy or rancher might have in the way of clothing or horse equipment. The Porter's of Phoenix catalog characterized those of the period. The company boasted that it supplied "almost everything necessary to ranch life except Bull Durham and a Lonely Hearts list."

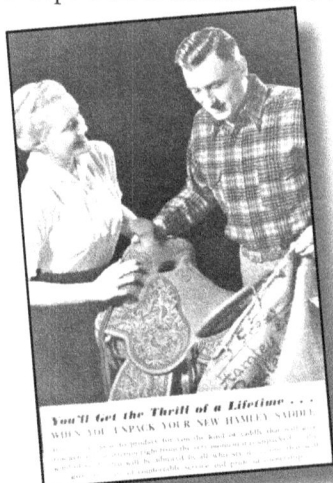

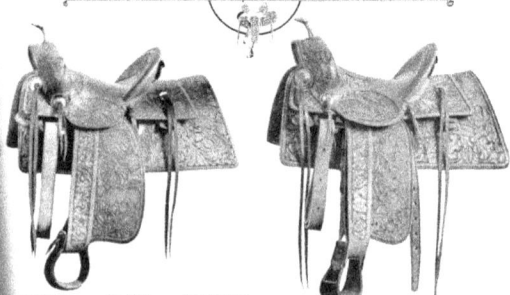

In the early catalogs, makers simply numbered their saddles for convenience in ordering. By the 1920s, however, many had begun to label each saddle with a distinctive name. For example, the 1924 Hamley Cowboy Catalog offered saddles named *Lamont, President, Favorite, Yakima, Strickland, Amarillo, Umatilla, Cody,* and *Hyannis.*

R.T. FRAZIER'S SADDLERY PUEBLO COLO.

The ad slogans employed by saddle makers in their catalogs rival anything one sees today coming from Madison Avenue's advertising agencies. For example, Hamley and Company stated that their saddles were "for men who care." Their 1924 Hamley Cowboy Catalog told readers that "Hamley Saddles talk for themselves through the people who ride them," while in 1939, the potential customer was assured that "You'll get the thrill of a lifetime when you unpack your new Hamley saddle."

Not to be outdone, the Visalia Stock Saddle Company's catalog for 1935 declared that "Visalia Quality is to Saddlery what Sterling Quality is to Silver." The Fred Mueller Saddle and Harness Company, in referring to its product, used "Man to Man—Here's Saddle Satisfaction," and urged customers to "Stick to the Fred Mueller Saddle." Their 1932 catalog stated, "The purchase of a celebrated Mueller saddle, harness, chaps, etc, is a good investment and not an experiment. They have stood the test since 1889, and our prices are the lowest in the West."

Some companies felt obliged to list every kind of item they made or sold either on the cover or title page of their catalogs. The 1927 Miles City Saddlery Company catalog is a typical example. It stated on the cover that they were "Dealers in fancy bits and spurs, stock saddles and harness, tents, tarpaulins and slickers, horse furnishing goods, cowboy boots and hats, Montana art, and leather goods."

In addition to ordering information, illustrations of the product line, and an index, each catalog invariably included a history of the company and a biography of its founder(s), plus photographs of its shops and employees. An invitation was also extended to the reader to visit the company's shop whenever the opportunity might arise.

Periodically, some makers featured informative articles in their catalogs such as "Do You Know How to Tie a Honda Loop? Here's How" which appeared in the 1924 edition of the Hamley Cowboy Catalog and "The 'Why' of a Cowboy's Wardrobe," a four-page piece included in the 1929-30 Porter catalog.

Some cowpunchers developed intense loyalties to particular companies, their product line, and their catalogs—to the exclusion of all others. Not only would these men buy each new saddle from a favorite company, but also clothing and other equipment, since they believed that their favorite firm supplied goods unquestionably the finest in style and quality when compared to the all others. The fact that almost all manufacturers carried the same lines of Stetson hats, Justin boots, Crockett and Kelly Bros. spurs, and Levi's overalls in their catalogs mattered little to these die-hard loyalists. These same men felt particularly honored when the letters and photographs they sent in praise of a new saddle or other piece of equipment appeared in their next catalog.

While saddle manufacturers geared their catalog products to the needs of cowboys and ranchers before World War II, they altered that approach afterward for several reasons. For one, cattlemen increasingly began using pickups, trailers, and stock trucks on their ranches which resulted in fewer horses being used, and consequently, fewer stock saddles being purchased.

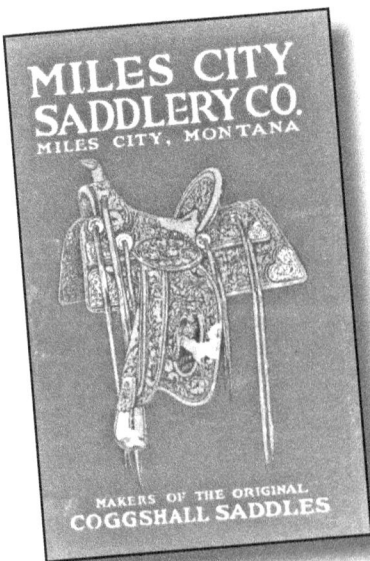

At the same time, post-war America began visiting Western dude ranches and attending rodeos in ever growing numbers. The style of dress for these activities was, of course, Western. As a result, companies like Hamley and Porter broadened their catalog lines by emphasizing clothing, especially women's apparel, to offset the decline in saddle sales. Significantly, in the late 1940s and through the 1950s companies placed their offerings of hats, boots, shirts, pants, and neck scarves in the front of their catalogs, where before

R.T. FRAZIER'S SADDLERY PUEBLO COLO.

CHAPAREJOS

No. 4212   Price $20.00   No. 4213   Price $18.00   No. 4214   Price $18.00

they had reserved that space for their line of saddles, which had been the cornerstone of their business.

Some firms eventually went entirely into selling Western wear, while those companies that continued to offer saddles often decreased the number of available styles. Generally speaking, catalogs issued after World War II consisted of fewer pages than those of previous years. This has resulted in the older catalogs becoming collectors' items.

Most of the well-known saddle manufacturing companies from the open range days have long since ceased operation. They have been succeeded by a number of production-line retail and wholesale outfits, as well as several custom shops boasting a few well-respected craftsmen working at the bench. Many of these contemporary craftsmen are carrying on the tradition of their predecessors by issuing mail order catalogs for future generations of cowboys to read, whether they need a saddle or not.

Makings: The Cowboy's Roll-Your-Own

R eading through the remembrances of old time cowboys one finds that most of them smoked cigarettes. Although manufactured cigarettes first appeared in the 1880s, most riders rolled their own up until World War II using predominately Bull Durham tobacco. Bull Durham was a product of the W.T. Blackwell Company's Durham Tobacco Works in Durham, North Carolina, which was established at the beginning of the Civil War.

Ramon Adams, who spent a lot of time at cow camps and ranches in the Southwest in the old days observing the habits of cowboys, commented in his book, *The Cowman Says It Salty,* that "if there ever was a badge of a calling it should be the little Bull Durham tag hanging by its yellow string from the vest or shirt pocket. I have heard several descriptions of a cowboy preparing to roll a smoke such as 'He strolled outside with a bag of Bull Durham in one hand while he gophers through his vest for papers with the other' and 'He jerked a leaf out of his prayer book (what he calls his book of cigarette papers) and commenced building a new life of Bull Durham.'"

The Blackwell Company's primary product came in either a two or four ounce white cotton sack with a yellow draw string tie that was used to secure the sack closed once the tobacco was poured out. In addition, a small

circular cardboard tag imprinted with the company's logo was attached to the string and served as a finger hold to pull the string tight. Often the cowpunchers pulled the sack closed by grabbing the string with their teeth.

The Blackwell Company also attached a package or book of brown rolling papers to each sack, which the cowboys sometimes called a "dream" or "prayer book." The reason for these names has been lost to history. Altogether the cowboys referred to the sack and papers as "makings," whereas the act of rolling a cigarette was called "twisting a cigarette" or "filling a blanket." Common slang terms for cigarettes themselves included "quirly," "pill," and "brain tablet."

Adams also observed that "when something was eating on a man and he was worried, he rolled a 'pill.' When he was embarrassed, he rolled a 'pill.' In fact, you'd find him building a smoke whenever he found his hands free to do the job." Adams wrote that whenever a cowpuncher ran out of makings, he could always ask "another rider for them, and they were never refused, unless the refusal was an intentional insult."

The Bull Durham tobacco sack also contained another benefit. Eugene Manlove Rhodes, the cowboy writer from New Mexico, related to his biographer that the sacks contained coupons that could be redeemed for paperback copies of *Munro's Library of Popular Novels,* free and postage paid from George Munro's Sons in New York. The book company offered a wide selection of titles that included works by Charles Dickens, Alexander Dumas, Robert Louis Stevenson, and Jules Verne. Aside from the literary value of the paperbacks, Rhodes liked them because they were small enough to fit in a leggings or saddle pocket. He further stated that almost all of the cowpunchers read them and often traded them with their friends for titles they had not read.

The cowpunchers rarely threw empty tobacco sacks away. They kept them to store all kinds of treasures and collections, but also gave them to women and kids of their acquaintance for the same purpose. Many men carried their Bull Durham in their front shirt pocket, but more often they used a pocket of their vest which was generally of "the ordinary, civilian type and usually worn unbuttoned." Cowboy chronicler, Phillip Ashton Rollins, wrote that vests were "worn not as a piece of clothing, but solely because its outside pockets gave handy storage not only to matches but also to makings."

In his book *The Cowboy* Rollins described the matches that a man carried in his vest as "like all matches on the range they came in thin sheets like coarsely toothed combs. They had small brown or blue heads that were slow to start a blaze and, for some time after striking, merely bubbled and emitted strong fumes of sulphur. To obtain a light the man tightened its trousers by raising its right knee and then drew the match across the trousers' seat."

The Diamond Match Company of Connecticut improved the sulphur match by fabricating it on a wooden stick in the early 1880s, which greatly facilitated not only lighting cigarettes but lamps and wood cook stoves as well.

Not every one on the range enjoyed smoking. Jack Culley, an Englishman who managed the Bell Ranch in New Mexico in the early 1890s, wrote in his book *Cattle, Horses, and Men* that "there were fellows I've known who never used a cuss word, or touched a drink or used tobacco. The usual smoke consisted of a granulated preparation whose name was reputed to have cost a million dollars a word to put on the market and which was said to be tobacco. This was poured into a brown 'cigareet' paper and lighted with a sulphur match which would choke you if you weren't careful. I could never get anything out of one of them except a lung full of sulphur, a whiff of smoke, and a taste of burnt brown paper. I smoked a pipe and like most all the fellows chewed *Star* and *Climax* plug."

Whereas Rollins commented that "eating and spitting tobacco was in common but far from universal use," Ramon Adams observed that cowpunchers "did not have much taste for a pipe, but left that tobacco furnace to the sheepherder, the nestor, and the prospector."

Another popular brand of sack tobacco was *Duke's Mixture* which was also manufactured and sold in Durham, North Carolina, by Washington Duke. Marty Robbins referred to *Duke's* in his popular song, "Cowboy in the Continental Suit," which is the story of an unlikely looking bronc rider who rode a horse called "The Brute."

> Well he said he came to ride the horse
> The one they called "The Brute,"
> But he didn't look like a cowboy
> In his continental suit.
>
> We knew he was a thoroughbred
> When he pulled his sack of "Duke's"
> From the inside pocket
> Of his continental suit.
>
> Well, he rolled himself a quirly
> And he lit it standing there.
> Blew himself a smoke ring and
> He watched it disappear.

At some point and for whatever reason "Duke's Mixture" came to refer to any odd combination of things or a strange mixture of items, especially relating to dogs.

Regarding rolling cigarettes, Rollins observed that "although the majority of cowboys had to use both hands in the operation of rolling and lighting, consummate elegance dictated that but a single hand be employed and that the rolling should be effected by the fingertips of this single hand." The smoke was finished by licking it with the "tongue along the paper cylinder," and the sack was closed by holding

the "finished cigarette…between the 4th and 5th fingers of the rolling hand" while "the thumb and forefinger of that hand grasped one loop of the tobacco sack's draw string" and "the puncher's teeth seized the other loop." Finally, "a match was drawn by the same rolling hand across the tightened trousers, and the cigarette was 'working.'" Cowboy folk lore tells that some men were so proficient at rolling cigarettes that they could do it while riding a pitching horse. Whether true or not, there are frequent references to cowpunchers who rode broncs without the ever present cigarette ever leaving their mouth.

The Montana cowboy artist Charles Russell recounted such an event in his book *Trails Plowed Under*. In the story "Bronc Twisters" Russell told about Charlie Brewster, who in his estimation was "one of the best that ever stepped across a hoss an' many a bad one he'd tamed." Charlie was with a roundup crew, riding a young roan horse when he...

> drops his hackamore reins an' builds a cigarette. Most men ridin' a hoss like his roan would be careful, but it's different with Charlie. He don't fear no hoss on earth, an' he ain't askin' no bronc whether he objects to smokin'. While he's rollin' his smoke the roan drops his ear down an' shows the white of his eyes, so it's easy to guess his feelin's is hurt. Charlie strikes a match, but he never lights his cigarette. While he's cuppin' his hands over the match, lettin' the sulphur burn off, somethin'—mebbe the brimfire sniff he gets—wakes the hell in the roan. He kicks the lid off, hides his head an' starts for the rimrock.

The bronc proceeds to buck off the edge of a nearby cliff, and Charlie's partners ride up, thinking all they'll see is a mass of cowboy and horse at the bottom of the canyon. To their surprise they see instead Charlie calmly sitting his horse securely lodged in the top of a cottonwood tree. When Charlie sees his friends looking over the rim rock at him, he nonchalantly asks, "Anybody got a match? The one I struck blowed out."

Typical wall advertisements for Bull Durham, Kit Carson, Colorado, 1880s.

The Blackwell Company was purchased by the Union Tobacco Company in 1898. Union continued to manufacture the Bull Durham brand until it consolidated into the group of companies comprising The American Tobacco Company. This firm continued production until 1989 when they discontinued the brand due to poor sales, stating that not enough people were rolling Bull Durham to warrant further effort. Today, although there is a pipe tobacco marketed as Bull Durham, about the only place one can buy a full sack of it is a few rare historic survivors being sold on the Internet.

Hat Etiquette

Ever since John Stetson started making beaver felt hats for western travelers more than 100 years ago, much has been written about the use and versatility of western head wear. In that venerable tradition, here are some observations based on casual encounters with ranch cowboys working on outfits in Texas, New Mexico, and Arizona over the last thirty years or so.

First of all, I have never seen a cowpuncher take a drink from the brim of his hat. He usually uses a cup or glass. Nor have I ever seen a horse take a drink from a hat full of water, as depicted in the old movies and shoot-'em-up novels. I have, on the other hand, seen men use their hats to fan a fire. Sometimes riders even use their hat to fan a pitching horse, although most of the men riding in such situations usually have other things on their mind.

Everyone knows that cowboys wear hats for, among other reasons, protection—from sun, rain, snow, wind, brush, trees, and hail. Men caught in hailstorms have been proud they were wearing hats and not baseball caps.

I know that a lot of good hands wear baseball caps when horseback. The problem is, when doing so, they don't enjoy the

Curtis Fort

R. W. Hampton

same protection that hats provide. I guarantee that if you get frapped (bucked off) on your head, you'd rather be wearing a hat than a baseball cap.

A lot of men wear baseball caps in the house or when in camp simply because they're used to having something on their head. But they will put their hat on if they drive to town to get the mail or take the wife shopping.

A note here—a cowboy never refers to his hat as a "cowboy hat." That would be redundant. Only people who are not cowboys, or who know nothing about cowboys, refer to them in such a manner. It's the same way with boots.

As far as color, by and large cowboys only wear two colors of hats— black or silver belly (which is light gray). Some wear only black, while others wear only silver belly. Some switch back and forth based on personal whim. Any other color is out, although I admit that I've seen some pretty good hands wear some shade of brown.

Cowpunchers generally aren't into fancy ribbons, bands, or brim bindings on their sombreros. They never wear feathers. Usually they don't wear a band on a "using" hat, which is the one they wear for riding or working. They might, however, put a rawhide or braided horsehair band on a town hat. Most men only own two hats—a town hat and a using hat (which used to be their town hat). Old hats that are no longer serviceable are given to kids or to dudes if they want them.

By looking at their hats you usually can tell ranchers or men who own ranches from the men who work on ranches. It depends a lot on whether the rancher or owner does work on the ranch. Most often, the man who owns the ranch but lives in town owns a more expensive hat than the man who works on the ranch.

Doug Johnson, WS Ranch

As in the old days, you can still tell a cowpuncher from Texas or New Mexico from a cowboy on the northern plains or a buckaroo from Nevada or Oregon by the shape of the brim of the hat and the crease in the crown. Saddle shops and western wear stores sell hats with generic cattleman creases in them. Nonetheless, it's often what a man does to the brim or crown of a hat while wearing it that demonstrates his vocation and where he's from. Often a man will wear the same crease that he started out with as a kid, and he'll keep wearing that type of crease for the rest of his life.

But that isn't always the case. Some men only buy hats with open crowns and then have them shaped by the folks at the store,

Jiggs Porter & Shorty Murray, CS Ranch

who will benefit from the new owner's coaching and advice about how the finished product should look. Other cowboys take their new hats back to the ranch uncreased. Then they either put them in the horse tank or steam them over boiling water to crease the hat themselves. To these discriminating riders, it is exacting work not to be left to others.

The rules of hat etiquette are unwritten, but like other similar rules they are taught and passed down through succeeding generations. When a cowboy enters a church or someone's house, he takes off his hat. A cowboy never eats in a café or restaurant with a hat on, unless he is eating solely with other men wearing hats. These days, few restaurants in cow country (or for that matter hotel lobbies, churches, banks, or theaters) are equipped with hat racks. This presents a problem for the man who wants to find a safe place to put his hat when he's required to take it off. Cowboys never put hats on beds. It's bad luck. That's why cowpunchers are reluctant to give up their hat to a city woman when entering her home, for fear of where she might put it.

When meeting or being introduced to a woman, some men tip their hat by grasping the brim, while others take it all the way off. In any event, propriety requires that you do one or the other. In the old days, cowboys never wore hats when dancing. Today, however, the rule is more relaxed. Generally these days only those men over 50 or 60 will take off their hats when asking a woman to dance.

It's easy to tell a city puncher from a cowboy by his hat. The city man doesn't usually treat his hat

Rod Taylor, Philmont Ranch

Boss Sanchez, Philmont Ranch

with the same care as a cowboy, perhaps because he doesn't wear it for its protective value. Even if a cowboy's hat has seen many trails in all sorts of weather, he attempts to maintain the hat in as close to its original shape as possible. It helps to maintain that shape by never setting down a hat on its brim. Dudes are always throwing theirs down on a table top or other flat surface, which causes an embarrassing flip on the back of the brim. The back of the brim also gets bent upward from rubbing against the headrest in a pickup. A cowboy wouldn't be caught dead with his hat like that. Besides, when hats are like that, they don't shed water like they're supposed to.

Many men wear straw hats in the summer. They are cooler than felt, but cowboys who work in the mountains or higher elevations hardly ever spend the money for a straw hat. It's not worth the expense for no more time than you get to wear it. Straw hats also blow off more easily in the wind, and they don't hold up very well when you have to ride hard through brush and timber.

I think it would be good if hats could talk.
Because of their vantage point,
they would have much to tell.

Parker & Marshall Zimmer

70

Roundup Beds

"Tired horses and tired cowboys make the best ones."
--Jiggs Porter

During the trail drives of the 1870s and '80s, cowboys commonly slept in pairs, each using his own blankets but sharing a doubled wagon sheet as protection against the elements. Once the ranges of the West were stocked, however, and cattlemen sent out roundup crews with chuckwagons to do the spring and fall work, cowpunchers began rolling their blankets inside individual canvas tarpaulins to make what they called roundup beds. Also referred to as hot rolls, flea traps, or shakedowns, they were not only comfortable, but could be counted on to keep a man warm and dry under almost any range conditions.

Roundup beds continue to be used today by cowboys working on ranches that run wagons and by many single men who live in bunkhouses or cow camps. Their prominent feature is portability because, although they are heavy and bulky compared to today's lightweight sleeping bags, they are easily rolled and thrown into a chuckwagon or pickup, or packed on a horse. No matter where a cowboy may travel or for what purpose, he can always have his personal bed with him.

The preferred tarpaulin, or tarp, for a roundup bed has traditionally been seven feet wide and eighteen feet long, made of waterproofed white ducking weighing eighteen ounces to the square yard. Rings are spaced along the sides of one end and snaps are sewn to the other. Canvas is used because it sheds water and is strong and durable.

When a cowpuncher hears the boss say, "Roll your bed," he knows he's been fired.

71

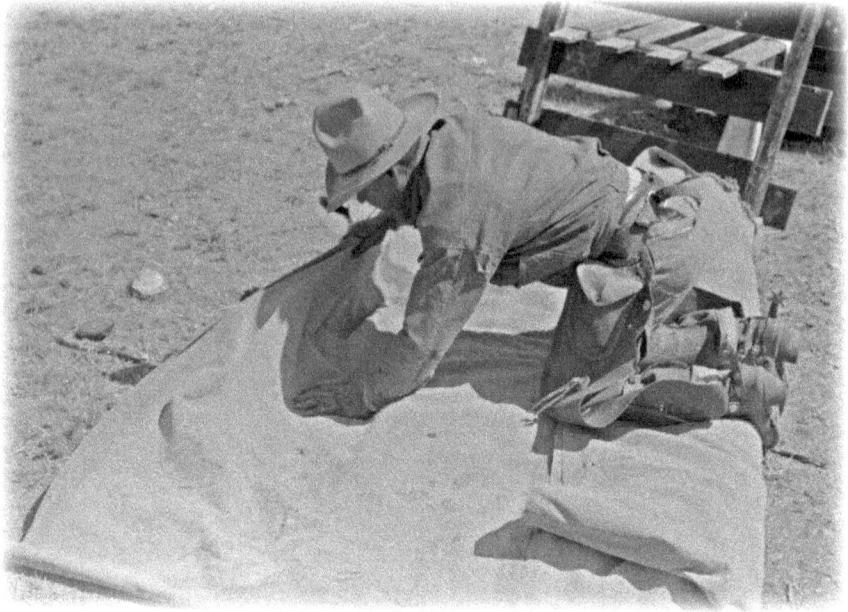

The tarp's length allows it to be folded in half over the bedding, thus protecting the blankets on both top and bottom. The edges can be fastened with the snaps and rings and, in case of rain or snow, they may be tucked under to keep everything dry inside.

Formerly, cowboys used doubled quilts called soogans for their bed's mattress, and they slept between light cotton blankets that were wrapped with heavier wool ones. Because of the greater frequency of inclement weather, riders in northern cowboy country necessarily required more blankets than their counterparts in the south, so northern bedrolls were considerably larger. As a result, a separate wagon was often needed on northern roundups to carry the outfit's beds.

Today, cotton or foam mattresses are popular, which makes the modern cowboy's bed bulkier and heavier, but arguably more comfortable. The man sleeps between conventional cotton sheets, with some preferring conservative white while others sport bright colors, stripes, or floral prints.

Because of where roundup beds are used, they easily become damp and dirty, making for extremely unpleasant sleeping. As a result, cowpunchers take every opportunity to wash their sheets and air out their tarps and blankets. Like any man's work, punching cows goes better after a good night's rest in a clean bed.

A rolled-up bed can be bound with a rope, which might be a worn lariat, or with two saddle latigos equipped with buckles. Many cowboys use latigos in case a spare one should be needed when out with the wagon or in camp.

During roundup each man is responsible for rolling his own bed and preparing it for loading in the wagon by the cook or horse wrangler. Should a rider be remiss at this chore, he could be fairly certain that his bed would be left behind when it came time for the cook to move the wagon to the next camp.

In the days before the West was fenced, most cowboys owned two or more private mounts with which they traveled from one ranch job to the next. One horse was ridden while another carried the man's bed and personal belongings. In order to pack a bed on a horse, the blankets were first folded and placed in the center of the spread-out tarp. The tarp's long edges were then folded over and the snaps fastened to the rings. Finally, the ends were brought together in the middle to cover the snaps. The bed was then lifted onto the horse's back, centered, and secured either with a W-hitch, S-hitch, or stirrup hitch—similar hitches that required a man on either side of the horse to tighten the

An unrolled bed frequently was used as a playing surface for a friendly game of cards or craps.

ropes. There was also a one-man hitch that allowed a solitary cowboy to tie the bed on by himself.

A roundup bed serves functions beyond simply a place to sleep. It could also be a suitcase where extra clothes are stored between the blankets, thus remaining clean, dry, and wrinkle-free. It is also the cowboy's safe deposit box which holds his war bag—a sack containing such personal effects as reading and writing materials, letters, tobacco, money, cards, and perhaps a spare bit or spurs. It is easy to understand why it might be unwise for a man to be caught prowling through another's bedroll.

The cowboy bedroll has provided the inspiration for many words and phrases common to range vernacular. For example, roundup time is sometimes referred to as "beddin' out" because it is when the men are required to sleep outside in their roundup beds.

When a cowpuncher is told by the boss to "Roll your bed," he knows he's been fired and must leave the outfit immediately. On the other hand, when the entire crew hears "Roll the cotton" or "Spool your beds," they know it is simply time to move camp. An overnight visitor to a roundup camp who has no bed is invariable offered a share of someone else's. The obliging rider will extend his invitation by saying he'll "split the blankets" or "cut the bed" with the guest.

Men accustomed to sleeping out on the range generally develop a certain routine in dressing and undressing. Charles Russell described the peculiarity of it in "The Story of a Cowpuncher" from his book *Trails Plowed Under*. After a night on the town, two strangers awaken one morning in a small hotel room in Chicago. One immediately determines that the other is a cowboy by watching him get dressed.

> Now humans dress up an' punchers dress down. When you raised, the first thing you put on is your hat. Another thing that shows you up is you don't shed your shirt when you bed down. So next comes your vest an' coat, keeping your hindquarters covered till you slide into your pants, an' now you're lacing your shoes. I notice you done all of it without quittin' the blankets, like the ground's cold...You've slept a whole lot with nothin' but sky over your head.

At the turn of the twentieth century, every saddlemaker who issued a catalog offered bed tarps for sale. Today, however, good tarps are not as easy to find. Fewer companies are sewing them, primarily because demand for them is not what it once was. With fewer ranches running wagons, fewer cowboys need roundup beds.

Sheridan Tent and Awning in Wyoming is at present one of the largest suppliers in the West for tarps used as roundup beds. They have made them along with range teepees, wall tents, and other canvas products, for more than 60 years. On average they sell 75 to 100 tarps a year, and although other companies often make them out of lighter weight canvas, Sheridan continues to make them from 18-ounce duck. Other firms selling good cowboy bedroll tarps include J.M. Capriola Company in Elko, Nevada, Tip's Western Wear and Custom Saddles in Winnemucca, Nevada, and Soda Creek Industries in Steamboat Springs, Colorado.

Sheridan reports that in recent years sleeping bag covers equipped with zippers and made of the same canvas have gained in popularity with many cowboys, packers, and hunters. Consequently, they don't sell as many bed tarps as they did in the past. Some cowboys today find they can make a more versatile bed by combining lighter synthetic or down sleeping bags with the durable canvas cover of a roundup bed.

The men who own traditional roundup beds, however, wouldn't trade them for any other kind. They value them almost as much as they do their saddles, and they wouldn't think of going out with the wagon or to a roundup camp without taking along their old roundup bed.

Cowboy Repair Box

During a visit to western sculptor Curtis Fort's studio awhile back, I noticed a wooden box sitting on a shelf in his saddle house. What caught my eye was the number of brands that were burned into the top and sides. When I asked Curtis about it, he told me that it held the leather-working tools he had collected over the last thirty years, whereas the brands represented a lot of the ranches he rode for during the same time. As we rummaged through the contents, Curtis spoke with fond memory about a number of the tools inside, telling me when he acquired or made a certain tool and what ranch he was working for at the time.

Like cowboys everywhere, Curtis discovered while growing up on the ranch his father managed near Tatum, New Mexico, that it was not always convenient to get to a saddle shop when a saddle needed repair. Even if a man could get to town, money was often needed elsewhere, and a cowboy had to make do by repairing things himself. As a result, Curtis learned from his dad how to do a lot of saddle and bridle repairs using a variety of tools ranging from a draw knife to a rivet setter. Importantly, his dad gave him an appreciation for doing each job in such a way that it would not only last, but look good as well.

He remembers going with his father to Ammonet Saddlery in Roswell to get a supply of latigo and leather skirting scraps that his dad would use to make saddle and bridle repairs. His dad also periodically bought a half-hide of leather or latigo from the shop so that he could cut bridle reins and make his own headstalls. When he needed to make such things, he showed Curtis how to cut them out of the hide and fin-

ish them off by using an edger to trim the sharp edges from the reins and bridles.

Curtis left home after high school to punch cows at the Pitchfork Ranch in Texas. In his outfit he included a sack filled with leather scraps along with a deer horn awl and a hole punch which he kept in his bedroll. These items, coupled with a sharp pocket knife, made possible most immediate repairs to his saddle and bridles while out with the wagon. Like he told me, the wagon boss could not afford to hold up the works waiting for a man to go town to get something fixed.

Following his first year of college, Curtis went to work for the Bell Ranch in northeastern New Mexico. Leo Turner was the Bell wagon boss, and from him Curtis learned several new ways to splice broken reins and make horn knots, among other things. Leo had punched cows for thirty years and as a result had accumulated a set of leather-working tools that he stored in what he called his treasure box. Curtis remembers how impressed he was with the contents, which included a drawknife, edger, hammer, lacing strings, heavy thread, beeswax, rivets, conchos, spur and bridle buckles, cinch rings, whetstones, and various stamping tools.

Seeing Leo's treasure box inspired Curtis to expand his own set of leather-working tools so that he could do more repairs and make new gear to add to his outfit. Leo helped by giving him an awl that he made from the tine of a hay rake. Together they found a piece of steel in the ranch shop and made a rivet setter that Curtis still uses today. Under Leo's direction, Fort's first effort at a leather project was a pair of brush cuffs. He decorated them by drawing a cow's head which he embossed on the leather, finishing them off with shiny steel spots.

At first Curtis stored his growing set of tools in a discarded bread tin that he found in the Bell Ranch junk pile. Some years later, however, he decided to build a box like Leo's to store his own tools. He found some scrap red cedar boards that came from a gate built for the boss' wife at the TX Ranch. Although he admits that he has never been much of a carpenter, he was pleased with his effort. He made a tray to sit inside the box which held the tools he used most often, and he decorated the outside of the box with his initials and the brands of the ranches for which he had worked.

He added an essential item to the outfit when he worked for the Vermejo Park Ranch in the early 1970s by fashioning a small anvil from a mine rail he found at an abandoned mining camp on the ranch. It was handy for setting rivets and for other repairs that required support when using a hammer.

As time went on during his cowboy career, Curtis enjoyed teaching the younger cowpunchers he worked with to make certain things and repair their equipment as he himself had been taught. He also showed them how to fancy up their bridles and chaps with conchos and steel spots. The cowboys were impressed with Curtis' box and its contents, just as he had been with Leo's box years before.

Although he now sculpts full time, he still gets horseback quite a bit helping his dad and neighbors around Tatum, especially at branding time. As a result, he continues to need the tools from his box just as he did during his active cowboy days. He keeps it stocked with conchos, buckles, lace leather, and heavy thread for whatever project he or anyone else might be working on. A similar box would be a handy idea for all horsemen, whether they are cowboys, pleasure riders, or trainers.

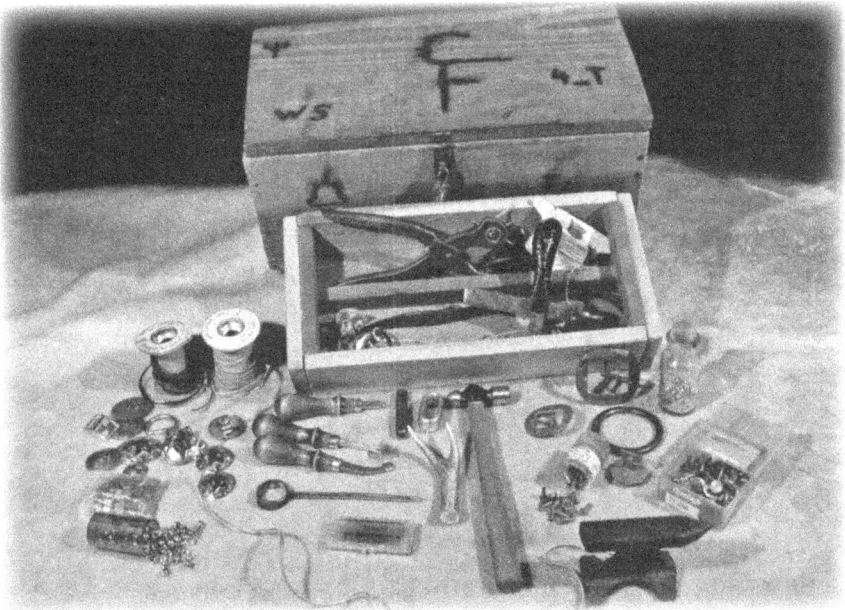

THE YOUTH'S COMPANION HISTORIC MILESTONES

KIT CARSON · · HUNTER AND TRAPPER · ·
IMPLACABLE FOE OF HOSTILE INDIANS BUT
FRIEND AND PROTECTOR OF THOSE THAT
WERE PEACEFUL · · TRAIL MAKER · PATHFINDER ·
GUIDE · · INCOMPARABLE SCOUT AND LOYAL AND
EFFICIENT SOLDIER · · THE LAST OF THE OLD FRONTIERS-
MEN AND ONE OF THE GREATEST

Kit Carson's Long Rides

K it Carson probably saw more of the American West from the back of a horse or mule than any mountain man or army officer of his time. Every year after he came to Taos in 1826, Carson ventured on a trapping expedition that took him to the far reaches of the Great Plains and Rocky Mountains. In the early 1840s he guided Colonel John C. Fremont on three western exploring expeditions, the second and third of which went as far a California.

The last expedition coincided with the beginning of the Mexican War, and Fremont's men were involved in taking possession of California for the United States. Afterward, Carson was sent on three cross-country trips to carry military dispatches and mail for officials in Washington, D.C., three thousand miles away. On each journey his men and animals encountered incredible hardships as they crossed the deserts and mountains in their path. Their efforts were frequently made more perilous by hostile Indian attacks.

On all three expeditions Carson primarily used mules for both riding and packing. From long experience he knew that not only could they travel longer distances on less forage and water than horses, but their greater endurance allowed them to better withstand the duress of forced wilderness travel.

Carson's first cross-country trip in the fall of 1846 was to be accomplished in sixty days. He left the pueblo of Los Angeles on September 5th with fifty mules and fifteen men, including six Delaware Indians, and headed across the Mojave Desert. When he reached the Colorado River, Carson crossed his cavalcade and led it up the Gila River in a forced march. Along the way he had to leave behind thirty-four mules that broke under the swift pace. Fortunately, he was able to acquire a few serviceable mounts from some Apache Indians that he encountered, although he had to trade two-for-one for most of them.

Thirty days after beginning his journey he reached the Rio Grande in New Mexico after traveling over 900 miles. South of Socorro he unexpectedly met General Stephen Watts Kearny who commanded the Army of the West. Two months earlier Kearny had taken possession of the Mexican province of New Mexico for the United States and was at the time on his way to confront Mexican forces in California.

After discussing the situation in California with Carson, Kearny asked the mountaineer to hand over his dispatches and return with him to California. He reasoned that because his current guide did not know the route across the desert as well as Carson did, military dictates demanded that Carson alter his plan. Carson was vexed over not being able to carry out his assignment but reluctantly agreed to pilot Kearny back across the desert.

Kearny left 200 of his troops in New Mexico so he would have a smaller force that could travel more rapidly to California. He mounted the remaining 100 Dragoons and twenty-one officers of his command on mules, although he himself chose to ride horseback. In addition, he brought along six ox carts drawn by eight mules each to carry the expedition's baggage.

Soon Carson realized that the carts greatly impeded the expedition's progress and convinced Kearny to leave them behind. The soldiers packed all of the necessary baggage on mules for the rest of the trip. Afterward, the mules suffered tremendously from the heat and lack of water in the desert, although none as much as Kearny's horse who gave out, forcing the General to put his saddle on a mule.

When the column reached the Colorado River, they encountered a group of Mexican traders who were driving a herd of 500 horses from California to Sonora. Kearny acquired some of the horses for his men, most of whom were by this time afoot. Unfortunately, most of the new mounts were eventually abandoned because they were unable to hold up under the Kearny' relentless pace.

The troops arrived in southern California in early December. They were met by a larger Mexican force at San Pasqual east of San Diego and were forced to establish a defensive stronghold. Unfortunately, the position did not have enough water for their horses and mules, so most

Kit Carson statue at Fort Carson, Colorado.
Although artists depict Carson on horses, he typically rode mules on his long rides.

of them had to be turned loose. Eventually Carson and Lieutenant Edward Beale were sent on foot for reinforcements in San Diego, which they reached after great hardship. When a relief party was sent to rescue the beleaguered command, Carson stayed in San Diego to recuperate from his walk across the desert.

The next February he was again ordered to Washington with dispatches. He left on the 25th accompanied by Lieutenant Beale and ten mountaineers formerly of Fremont's command. Beale wrote in his journal that their mules suffered terribly from thirst on the trek across the desert before they reached the Colorado River. Afterward, they had to fight Apaches several times as they followed the Gila River in New Mexico, subsisting primarily on mule meat most of the way. They reached Santa Fe during the first week of April.

After a ten day stay in Taos to be with his wife, whom he hadn't seen in two years, Carson led his men east across the mountains to the Santa Fe Trail and north to the Purgatorie River. On his way to Bent's Fort on the Arkansas River, he met a young adventurer named Lewis Garrard who later wrote that several of Carson's men were dressed in California costume, and their "high pummeled saddles, large live-oak stirrups and

Kit Carson statue in Trinidad, Colorado.

huge iron spurs, a few inlaid with silver, the rowels four or five inches in diameter, formed a unique appearance."

At the mouth of the Purgatorie, Carson left seven of his men with the party's broken down mules so they might "recruit by rest and grass." At Bent's Fort he acquired fresh mounts. He continued along the Santa Fe Trail and arrived in St. Louis at the end of May having traveled two thousand miles in three months.

In St. Louis Carson bought store clothes to wear for the rest of the trip to Washington, although he soon found them confining compared to the buckskins he normally wore on the trail. His subsequent itinerary included passage by steamboat down the Mississippi and up the Ohio River followed by an overland stage to Washington where he arrived in early June.

Carson delivered his dispatches to the appropriate military officials and met with President John Polk to explain the affairs in California. On June 14th he was ordered to return west with dispatches for Colonel Sterling Price in Santa Fe and General Kearny in California. Before he departed, President Polk signed a commission proclaiming him a 2nd Lieutenant of the US Mounted Riflemen.

When Carson reached Fort Leavenworth in Kansas, he requisitioned mules for his overland trek and was given fifty raw infantry volunteers as an escort. Being a newly commissioned officer, he dressed in a Dragoon cap, wool trousers, and a long skirted coat for the trip across the Plains which was accomplished after only one altercation with Comanche Indians.

In New Mexico he turned over his dispatches to Colonel Price and recruited sixteen mountaineers to ride with him on the remainder of the trip to California. He changed into buckskins for the trail and opted to lead his men along the Spanish Trail to the Green River in present day Utah. He chose this route because the Gila Trail he had used previously had been left bare of forage by Kearny's earlier march.

Carson followed the Sevier River into present day Nevada where his party had to defend themselves against a band of Indian raiders. He later said in his memoirs that "I had no more trouble on the road, only having got out of provisions and had to eat two mules." Arriving at Los Angeles in October, Carson stayed there for the rest of the winter.

The following May he was sent for the third time with military reports and mail overland to Washington. Prominent within his pack was a copy of the *California Star* dated April 1, 1848, which contained an account of the discovery of gold at Sutter's Mill. Leading twenty-seven men, including Lieutenant George Brewerton, Carson left Los Angeles on May 4th. The expedition was again mounted on mules and drove a large remuda of extra mules and horses along with their pack mules.

Brewerton's involvement is noteworthy because he later wrote an account of the expedition's trek across the Spanish Trail titled *A Ride with Kit Carson*. It contains important details about their day-to-day life on the trail and much about the idiosyncrasies of the Spanish mules they rode and packed.

Brewerton wrote that many of the "men were noted woodsmen, old companions of Carson in his exploration with Fremont, while others...were almost as ignorant of mountain life as myself knowing nothing of the mysteries of a pack saddle and keeping at a most respectful distance from the heels of a kicking mule."

THE YOUTH'S COMPANION HISTORIC MILESTONES

KIT CARSON .. HUNTER AND TRAPPER .. IMPLACABLE FOE OF HOSTILE INDIANS BUT FRIEND AND PROTECTOR OF THOSE THAT WERE PEACEFUL .. TRAIL MAKER . PATHFINDER . GUIDE .. INCOMPARABLE SCOUT AND LOYAL AND EFFICIENT SOLDIER .. THE LAST OF THE OLD FRONTIERS. MEN AND ONE OF THE GREATEST

He described the order of march as being "Kit and myself, with one or more of our party came first, then followed the pack mules and loose animals, and in their rear the remainder of our men, who urged the mules forward by loud cries, and an occasional blow from the ends of their lariats. Our saddles were of the true Mexican pattern, wooden trees covered with leathers called macheers [*mochilas*]. This saddle for service I found far superior to those of American make, being both easier and safer, the great depth of the seat rendering it almost impossible for the animal to dislodge his rider, a fact which partly accounts for the fearless horsemanship for which Mexicans are so famous. Our bridles, formed of twisted hide or horse hair, were ornamented with pieces of copper and furnished with strong Spanish bits. As for our spurs, they were sharp and heavy enough to have driven an elephant, not to speak of a California mule, which I take to be the more unmanageable beast of the two."

Concerning dress, Brewerton reported that "I was attired in a check or 'hickory' shirt as they are called, a pair of buckskin pants, a fringed hunting shirt of the same material, gaily lined with red flannel and ornamented with brass buttons." He completed his outfit with cowhide boots and a broad-brimmed straw hat.

Brewerton wrote that the routine of desert travel had a "terrible sameness about it; we rode from fifteen to fifty miles a day, according to the distance from water; occasionally after a long drive halting for twenty-four hours, if the scanty grass near the camping grounds would

Unveiling of the Kit Carson statue on June 1, 1913, at Kit Carson Park in Trinidad, Colorado. One of Carson's daughters and two of his granddaughters were present at the ceremony.

permit it, to rest and recruit our weary stock...At night every care was taken to prevent surprise; then men took turns in guarding the animals, while our own mess formed the camp guard of the party. In an Indian country it is worthy of remembrance that a mule is by far the best sentry; they discover either by their keen sense of smell, or of vision, the vicinity of the lurking savage long before the mountaineer, experienced as he is, can perceive him. If thus alarmed, a mule shows its uneasiness by snorting and extending the head and ears toward the object of distrust."

Kit Carson sculpture atop the Denver Pioneer Monument.

Carson's third cross-country expedition arrived in Taos after forty-one days on the trail from California. He briefly reported to the military authorities in Santa Fe, discharging all but ten of his men, including Lieutenant Brewerton, and then embarked on a round-about trek across the Plains.

He had been alerted that Comanche Indians were closely watching traffic on the Santa Fe Trail through Kansas, and in order to avoid them he decided to lead his men north along the foot of the Rockies. When he reached the South Platte River, he went down it to Fort Kearny and from there along the Republican River to Fort Leavenworth. He arrived in St. Louis on July 31st and then made his way alone to Washington where he delivered his mail. He was back in New Mexico by October.

This was the last of Kit Carson's three long rides. It would be interesting to know how many saddles he rode and perhaps wore out on the three trips and in the course of covering roughly eight thousand miles. In all of the chronicles of long distance travel in the American West, Carson's exploits were never equaled.

The Pacing Black Mustang of Antelope Springs

R ange historian J. Frank Dobie had a great affinity for horses, especially the wild horses or mustangs which roamed the American West. Among the stories he collected in his celebrated book, *The Mustangs*, were those devoted to the courage, endurance, and beauty of several white stallions and their exploits in avoiding capture by mustangers. In these legendary frontier accounts most of the stallions escaped because they possessed a pacing gait that enabled them to outdistance their would-be captors.

A similar story, which Dobie described as "beautiful and true to range men as well as their horses," was gathered by naturalist Ernest Thompson Seton. Seton was wolf hunting on the L Cross F Ranch in northeastern New Mexico in the fall of 1893 when he became familiar with a mustang stallion of exceptional qualities. The story he heard differed from Dobie's accounts because this stallion was shiny coal-black instead of white, although he too was a natural pacer and had "thin, clean legs and glossy flanks."

Seton's pacing mustang was first observed as a yearling by a number of cowpunchers who made plans to catch him. Before anyone actually made an attempt, however, the colt had turned three years old and had taken charge of nine "half-blooded" mares who wandered away from the ranch. Initial efforts

Naturalist Ernest Thompson Seton

to gather the gentle mares were unsuccessful due to the black stallion's skillful handling of them. Soon a consensus was reached that the only way to get back the valuable mares was to either catch or kill the pacer. In December 1893 Seton set out from headquarters with the L Cross F wagon. The ranch manager told him, "If you get a chance to draw a bead on that...mustang, don't fail to drop him in his tracks."

The pacer was soon sighted by one of the cowboys. Seton took his rifle and climbed a ridge, expecting to take a shot, but the magnificence of the horse stopped him. He later wrote that the stallion "heard some sound of our approach, and was not unsuspicious of danger. There he stood with head and tail erect, and nostrils wide, an image of horse perfection and beauty, as noble an animal as ever ranged the plains, and the mere notion of turning that magnificent creature into a mass of carrion was horrible."

As a result of this encounter, Seton threw open the breech of his rifle. The cowboy with him reached for the gun, but Seton turned the muzzle to the sky and it "accidentally" went off. It was Seton's only sighting of the stallion, but while in New Mexico he heard other stories of attempts to capture that swift horse. He recorded some of them in his book of animal stories, *Wild Animals I Have Known*, which appeared in 1898.

One of those accounts tells about Wild Jo Calone, the cowpuncher who gave the most serious consideration to capturing the stallion. Most of his associates thought he was crazy to waste good men, horses, and time on an animal that probably had no value. However, when the owner of the Triangle Bar Ranch, in the presence of witnesses, offered a thousand dollars to anyone who could deliver the stallion safely to a boxcar, Wild Jo decided it was time to make his move.

With an outfit of twenty saddle horses, a mess wagon, cook, and a partner, he planned to walk down the mustang and his band. The mustanger's idea was to follow the stallion horseback at a leisurely pace until the horse got used to a trailing rider. Then Calone planned to continue to pressure the horse and wear him down so much that he would have little time to eat and drink. The cowpuncher then hoped to rush in and rope the stallion.

When all was ready Wild Jo led his outfit to Antelope Springs, the favorite watering place of the pacer and his band. When Calone's outfit spotted the stallion, the horse took alarm and led his mares away at a high lope across a nearby mesa. Jo quickly followed, and as he came upon them he slowed his horse to a walk. They ran again. The cowboy cut their trail at a trot as they circled to the south, and caught up with them after several miles. He again walked quietly toward the horses. When they took flight, Jo rode back to the wagon and arranged with the cook to meet at a place that would intersect with the horses' circle.

Wild Jo trailed the horses until dark and then switched with his partner, Charley, who took after the band on a fresh horse. By now the herd was getting used to the company of a trailing horseman. The horses did not run as far as they had at first. Charley walked after them for a few hours in the dark, aided not only by a sure-footed mount,

but also by a white mare in the band who was easily seen in the pale moonlight. Later Charley stopped, unsaddled, and lay down to sleep on his saddle blanket by his picketed horse.

At dawn Charley found the herd no more than half a mile away. They immediately bolted, moving westward. Charley soon saw the smoke of the outfit's camp, and when he reached it Wild Jo took over to trail the herd. This pattern was repeated for the next two days. The horses continued to move in a circle, destined eventually to bring them back to their favorite water. Although the horses progressively felt more at ease with their pursuers, the constant travel, even at a walk, was beginning to wear on them. The band began to suffer constant nervous tension from the day and night pursuit.

Whereas Jo's and Charley's horses ate grain twice a day, the mustangs had to graze on the run, instead of locating a good stand of grass and eating at their leisure. The stress also caused them to become unusually thirsty. Wild Jo allowed the wild band to drink as much and as often as they desired, knowing how a running horse filled with water would get stiff limbs and lose wind.

By the fifth day the herd had almost reached Antelope Springs. The mares began lagging, in spite of the black stallion's efforts to urge then on. Often they were no more than 100 yards ahead of the relentless, trailing horseman. Wild Jo's plan had been executed with only one hitch. Whereas the mares were done in, the pacer seemed to be as strong as when the chase began.

When they reached the springs, Jo kept the herd from water for a few hours and then let them drink their fill. He soon realized that he would probably not have to rope the mares, because he could easily separate them from the stallion and drive them back to the L Cross F corral. Jo directed his full attention to the pacer. For the final chase the cowboy caught his favorite and fastest mount, *Lightfoot*. Although she was of eastern blood, she had been raised on the plains and Jo was confident she had the bottom to catch the stallion.

Jo took after the stallion at a run. On discovering his pursuer, the mustang jerked up his head and started off at his usual swinging pace. Jo was a quarter of a mile behind, and using shouts and spurs, the cowboy urged the mare to lessen the stallion's lead. The mustang led Jo across a long, grassy stretch, still maintaining the same even gait. The cowboy was astonished that the distance was actually widening between them.

Then, suddenly, his mare went down, the victim of a badger hole. Jo went sprawling, but quickly jumped to his feet to remount. The courageous mare, however, had broken her right foreleg and Jo sadly put her down. As he carried his saddle back to camp, he could see the stallion striding off in the far distance.

All was not lost for Wild Jo and Charley, though. They claimed a sizable reward for the return of the L Cross F mares, but Jo never forgot the pacing black stallion of Antelope Springs.

Cattle Ranch to Polo Field

Polo is the fastest team sport in the world. It holds preeminence in speed because the legs of the player are those of the horse he rides. After its introduction to the United States in 1876, polo had gained well-deserved recognition as a national sport by 1920. Over the next two decades spectators by the thousands thronged to Eastern polo fields to watch the daring, wide-open play of high goal sportsmen mounted on horses of uncanny athletic ability and speed.

As the game developed in the United States, players increasingly refined the techniques of both individual and team play. Moreover, they brought to the game better bred and faster horses that dramatically increased the pace. Players demanded the fastest horses capable of playing the game—a fast horse meant reaching the ball before an opponent, or at the very least, maneuvering quickly to catch him out of position.

From the earliest years various cattle ranches throughout the West supplied a large number of horses for the game. A western cow horse was a natural, possessed of the intelligence, athletic ability, and courage necessary to play the game. Nevertheless, western cow horses were generally small, having descended from range mustangs and, consequently, were comparatively slow.

The thoroughbred racing horse did meet the players' requirements for speed. With the growing popularity of the sport and the demand for faster horses, many western cattlemen began bringing thoroughbred blood onto their ranches for the purpose of breeding up their brood bands and selling the outstanding offspring for the game of polo.

In the process, ranches found that any horses unable to make the grade for polo and other equestrian sports often made the best mounts for their cowboys to use in cattle work.

In 1930 Will Rogers, an enthusiastic proponent and player of polo, commented in his newspaper column that many of the polo ponies used by teams in the East had been bred and trained on western ranches. He felt that the game of polo had "done more to establish the breeding of good horses" in the West than even horse racing had.

Horse breeders in West Texas were at the vanguard of raising and training ponies for use by clubs in the East. In New Mexico, two large ranches situated at the foot of the Sangre de Cristo mountains near Cimarron followed suit by up-breeding their horse herds with the intent of marketing both young horses and seasoned mounts for polo, jumping, and the US Cavalry.

The CS Cattle Company, managed by Edward Springer, along with the neighboring Philmont Ranch, owned by Oklahoma oilman Waite Phillips, began raising thoroughbred and part-thoroughbred horses in the 1920s. When cattle prices plummeted at the outset of the Great Depression, these cattlemen accelerated their horse breeding programs and used them as sources of important income.

The economic incentives were substantial. Whereas a good cow horse might sell for $100 to $150 at the beginning of the Depression, a polo prospect—a young horse untrained for the game but having the proper conformation and breeding—might go for as much as $300, while a seasoned, well-trained mount would bring much more.

The famous CS Ranch pony, Breeches, *who competed on several Eastern polo teams.*

Both the CS and Philmont ranches made concerted efforts to promote their horses by advertising in various sports and horse-related publications. They also produced local polo shows and tournaments where the buying public could see firsthand the training and breeding of their horses. By the beginning of the Depression, the Springer thoroughbred and better-bred mares numbered over 200 head and were producing colts that displayed the conformation, disposition, and speed to make them capable of playing international polo, working cows, or serving in the cavalry.

The US Army's Western Remount Service aided the CS and Philmont breeding programs by allotting them seventeen thoroughbred stallions during the 1930s. In exchange for the services of these studs, each ranch agreed to sell certain horses from the resulting get to the Army for cavalry mounts. With its potential for bringing in additional revenue and for upgrading breeding herds, this program was popular on ranches throughout the West. Many of the horses selected were taken by officers as polo mounts and used by Army teams at posts scattered across the country.

1935 advertisement for the Cimarron Rodeo, featuring polo ponies.

Success in selling horses for whatever purpose depended not only on their breeding, but on skillfully handling them during the crucial period while they were still colts. Colts that demonstrated the disposition and conformation to make polo mounts were put to saddle as three-year-olds. After they responded to bridle and bit and had learned to handle their feet under the weight of a rider, they underwent preliminary training on the polo field to accustom them to the ball and mallet. In their fourth year they were ridden in slow practice games where they learned to play the game under the tutelage of a patient rider. In the meantime, they were often given to the ranch cowboys to develop as cow horses.

Some horses were sold in the fall of their first year of training. The more precocious, however, were held back for several seasons of subsequent play at which time they were sold for higher prices as seasoned polo mounts. Beginning in 1934 the CS and Philmont ranches inaugurated a series of horse shows in Cimarron to promote the sale of their horses. The first, held on June 17, 1934, drew 4,000 breeders, buyers, and spectators from all over the country. A full range of competitive events for polo, polo-prospect, and cavalry mounts were featured. A local men's group, the Cimarron Maverick Club, helped sponsor the event along with the United States Polo Association which donated $200 as the show's prize money. In addition to show events, a polo tournament was staged following the opening day performance, for the purpose of demonstrating the abilities of the horses rather than the talents of individual players or teams.

As a result of the success of the first Cimarron Polo Show, Waite Phillips donated a tract of land in Cimarron to the Maverick Club for a polo field, arena, and rodeo grounds. For his part, Ed Springer built nearby barns, club rooms, and other facilities. In the spring of 1935 the arena was prepared for another show in June.

Participation in the 1935 Cimarron Horse Show exceeded that of the previous year. The *Raton Range* reported that the 1935 show demonstrated again to "dealers and players East, West, and Far West that the ponies [in the Cimarron district] were capable of playing in the fastest company."

Late that summer Ed Springer of the CS Ranch, Roy Lewis, Philmont Ranch manager, and Brownlow Wilson of the WS Ranch and general manager of the 1935 show, established the Cimarron Polo Club. The club served as an official body to promote the sale of locally raised and trained polo ponies through sponsorship of polo games and horse shows.

To demonstrate the breeding and training of their polo ponies to a wider audience, the CS Ranch entered the Colorado Springs Broadmoor Hotel polo tournament in August 1936. The CS players won the finals of the Lyle Cup on August 11th at Penrose Park Field against a team sponsored by the Broadmoor Hotel. The Colorado Springs *Gazette* reported that the CS team rode "exceptionally fast mounts and as a result...outrode and outplayed the Broadmoor quartet." The next weekend the CS team again defeated the Broadmoor in the finals of the Penrose Polo Cup by a score of 10-8. The Broadmoor tournament marked the end of the polo season along the front range of the Rockies, and the play of the horses and riders from the CS drew further national attention to Cimarron's polo activities.

In the summer of 1937 a unique ranch was established south of Cimarron based on the village's reputation as a polo breeding and training center. Founded as the Vallejo Polo Ranch, its operation initially centered on schooling polo prospects for the game, but after a year of operation, it expanded to include a players' school where aspiring poloists could learn the fundamentals and horsemanship of the game.

The ranch founder, an English sportsman and poloist named W.L. Horbury, created a guest ranch atmosphere for the players, providing them with comfortable lodgings and varied leisure-time activities. Vallejo advertised with the slogan, "We train both man and horse," and urged potential students to combine instruction in polo form and fundamentals with a pleasant summer vacation.

By the end of the 1930s it seemed that the Cimarron district was destined to rival West Texas as the major polo pony breeding and training area in the United States. The CS and Philmont ranches continued producing horse shows and selling polo ponies in the pre-war years, but as fighting increased in Europe, more and more of their potential polo mounts were diverted for sale to the horse cavalry of the US Army as it prepared for possible deployment. American involvement in World War II dealt a crippling blow to polo nationwide as both players and horses were called up for military service and most clubs were disbanded.

After the bombing of Pearl Harbor, the CS turned its full attention away from horses toward cattle production to support the war effort. At the same time, the status of the Philmont Ranch changed. In late

Cimarron Polo Club on their playing field c. 1935.

1941 Waite Phillips deeded a major portion of the ranch to the Boy Scouts of America as a national wilderness camp that became Philmont Scout Ranch. The rest of the ranch was sold to an Arizona cattleman, while the majority of the Philmont mares were sold to outside breeders.

American polo has in recent year regained much of its popularity, and although the Cimarron ranches are no longer a part, many of the game's horses continue to be raised and trained in the West. Although scattered throughout the country, the CS and Philmont mares and stallions left an important legacy in the modern horse world. This legacy displays the same intelligence, athletic ability, and conformation of their forebears, and they have in their own right exhibited top performance not only on ranches but in national racing, cutting, and horse show events as well.

Will James

Will James was not only an acclaimed author and illustrator, but he was a working cowboy and, in essence, a contradiction. He got his start drawing pictures on his family's kitchen floor at age four, and during his 30-plus year career he wrote and illustrated twenty-three books. Little did he know that the verbal and visual documentations in his books, such as *Lone Cowboy*, would become icons of the American West and endearing chronicles of cowboy culture.

As a teenager James was a drifter, going from ranch to ranch in search of outdoor work. In the summer of 1907, at the age of 15, he left his home in Ontario, Canada, and headed for the cattle ranges of western Canada to live life as a cowboy. Three years later he crossed into the United States and ran wild horses in Idaho, then worked on several ranches in Montana and Wyoming. Along the way, he earned a reputation for two talents: riding broncs and sketching them. James drew broncs from the experience of riding them, rather than from watching someone else. He wrote that his inspiration came "thru my tail, and from the many connections it got with the cantle board of my saddle."

In the spring of 1914 James went to work for a northeastern Nevada

ranch. Discontented with the owners, he and a fellow cowpuncher drove off a bunch of the ranch's cows, intending to sell them. They loaded the cattle at Oasis, Utah, and James' partner boarded the train destined for Denver. James stayed to sell their horses, but as the only stranger in town he was soon accused of the theft and arrested. His partner escaped and sold the cattle, never being heard from again. James eventually was convicted of cattle rustling and sentenced to the Nevada State Prison, where he served a year before being released in April 1916 for good behavior.

Upon his prison release, James returned to riding horses. A few months later, a horse he was breaking kicked him in the mouth. In search of a qualified dentist to repair the damage, James headed to Los Angeles, California. To pay for the dental work and to occupy his time between treatments, he worked for a stable that supplied horses and riders for western movies. A natural in the saddle, James was soon performing in many films, not all of which were westerns, both as a horseback extra and as a stunt double.

Never one to stay anyplace for long, James returned to the Nevada range as soon as his dental treatments were finished. He then headed to Great Falls, Montana, to find work and seek the advice and critique of cowboy artist Charles Russell, whose paintings he'd admired for years.

Early sketch titled "The Nevada Mustang"

During the visit, Russell was engrossed in a painting project and virtually ignored James, beyond giving a cursory glance at the drawings he'd brought. Russell's only suggestion was that James spread his art around the saloons in hopes that someone would buy it there.

Leaving Montana discouraged, James returned to Nevada in the spring of 1918 and was drafted by the US Army. Stationed at Camp Kearney near San Diego, California, James served the remainder of World War I as a mounted scout. After his discharge, James returned to Nevada and teamed with two other cowboys to put on bucking-horse exhibitions in Reno, Nevada. James got bucked off a horse called Happy and struck his head on a railroad track, suffering a concussion that required hospitalization. With plenty of time to ponder his future, James recognized his bronc-riding days were probably over, but he still had his art.

Through the years many people had encouraged James to pursue an art career, so he decided to give it a try. First, he enrolled in the California School of Art in San Francisco. He attended classes for three months, but felt formal instruction thwarted his natural style. His first big break came when he showed some of his drawings to the editors of *Sunset* magazine. They liked his work and published one of the drawings, titled *A One Man Horse*, early the next year. They later used a series of his drawings, titled *Keno the Cow Horse: A Life Story in Pictures*, along with his explanatory notes.

Encouraged by this success, James sent a sketch to Russell and again asked for a critique. This time Russell replied positively and wrote, "I know you have felt a horse under you. Nobody can tell you how to draw a horse or a cow." He encouraged James to "keep on making real men and cows...the real artistick may never know you, but nature loving regular men will...an thair the kind you want to shake hands with."

In July 1920 James married Alice Conradt in Reno. Early the next year the couple left Nevada to work on a ranch near Kingman, Arizona. In hiring James, the ranch manager agreed to let him work on his art. James took the opportunity to use oils to paint bucking horses, as Russell advised him to do in his letter. Money was scarce, and Alice grew

103

*Will and Alice James
at the Washoe Valley ranch.*

uncomfortable with the isolation of the camp, so she returned to Reno to live with her parents.

To develop his budding art career, James moved to Santa Fe, New Mexico, to be near a thriving art colony. Although he sold a painting and was commissioned to do others, James still wasn't earning enough to support himself, so he began looking for another riding job. He met Wallace Springer, an art enthusiast who was from a pioneer New Mexico ranching family. Springer urged James to go to the ranch headquarters in Cimarron and ask his brother Edward for a job.

James spent the summer at the ranch's La Grulla cow camp in the mountains southwest of Cimarron. Later, Springer rode into camp with a friend, Burton Twitchell, a dean at Yale University. Twitchell was impressed with James and his ability to draw horses and tell stories. After conferring with Springer, Twitchell told James about an art scholarship at Yale that could be made available to him. Despite his past art school experiences, James was enticed by the idea because of the potential to meet New York magazine editors. Springer, for his part, agreed to fund James' living expenses.

James' experience at the Yale art school mirrored that in San Francisco. Once again, he became convinced that he couldn't benefit from instruction and soon withdrew. However, he stayed long enough to meet several magazine editors in New York, including the editor of *LIFE*, who liked his drawings but told him the magazine's editorial board had rejected them for publication. Feeling dejected, James returned to Reno uncertain about his future.

Sensing her husband's despair, Alice encouraged him to use his storytelling ability to write about his experiences on the range. Although skeptical, James decided it was worth a try. In one week he finished a story titled, "Bucking Horses and Bucking Horse Riders," and drew six sketches to illustrate it. He sent the story to *Scribner's* magazine in New York, which was one of the most popular magazines in America at the time. Although the story was written in cowboy vernacular, rather than the magazine's formal English style, the editors were sold on the illustrations. James was surprised and elated when the magazine quickly accepted the story and sent a check for $300.

James immediately began writing more stories based on his life on the range. In the next six months he wrote and illustrated seven more stories that Scribner's compiled into a book, *Cowboys North and South*. Proceeds from the book went toward buying five acres near Franktown, Nevada, where James built a house and studio.

This book drew nationwide praise. The *New York Herald Tribune* wrote that James had "done an exceedingly wise and artistic thing... [by writing] exactly as the average cowpuncher talks, and that gives his book a unique distinction among books of the Far West." Another newspaper praised James' drawings, writing that "his draftsmanship is as self-taught as his literary style, but in their vigor and truthfulness his studies of horses and cattle are extraordinarily good. They have nothing to fear from comparison with the work of Frederic Remington or any other artist of the Plains."

A year later, James had written and illustrated stories for another book titled *Drifting Cowboy*. One reviewer complimented the publisher for having "the good judgment not to translate the book into English." Scribner's editors next urged James to write a novel-length cowboy story. He spent the next year writing and illustrating his more famous book, *Smoky the*

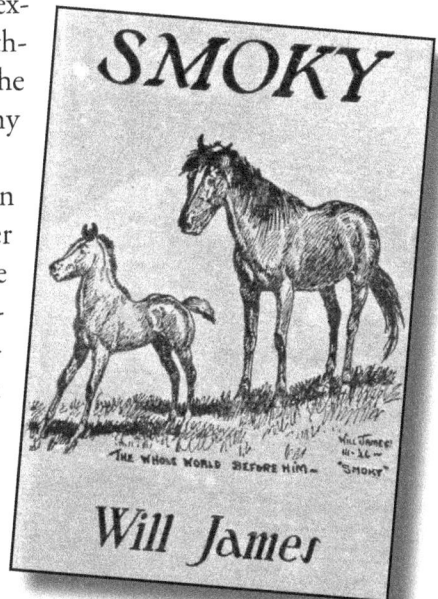

Cowhorse, patterned after his all-time favorite horse by the same name.

The novel was serialized in *Scribner's* beginning in April 1926, and it was later published as a book in September. It met with immediate success and was reprinted ten times in the next four months. The *New York Times* called it "the Black Beauty of the cow country." In 1927 the American Library Association awarded *Smoky* the Newberry Medal as the year's most distinguished contribution to American literature for children.

With the financial success of *Smoky*, James purchased a ranch south of Billings, Montana, in the foothills of the Pryor Mountains. By August 1927 he and Alice had established Rocking R Ranch, and over the next two years James wrote two more books, *Cow Country* and *Sand*. He then started writing his autobiography, which was a project he'd planned for some time. Writing five or six hours a day and drawing at night, James spent six months completing the book. Whereas James had handwritten his other books, he had Alice use a typewriter for the chapters of his life story. In doing this, she learned much about her husband's early years that she hadn't known before.

Lone Cowboy: My Life Story was issued on August 1, 1930, and received glowing reviews. In this book James wrote that he had been born in Montana where his parents were en route from Texas to start a ranch. His mother died within a year, and his father was gored and killed by a bull four years later. Jean Beaupre, a French-Canadian trapper and friend of his father, took charge of the boy and taught him the ways of the wilderness. Tragedy struck again when the trapper drowned. Undaunted, the 15-year-old boy gathered his belongings and found a ranch where he started his cowboy career.

James provided few details in the book about the ranches where he worked, and a noted western artist, Ross Santee, took exception with this lack of detail. He chided James by writing that "states have names and when a cowboy works

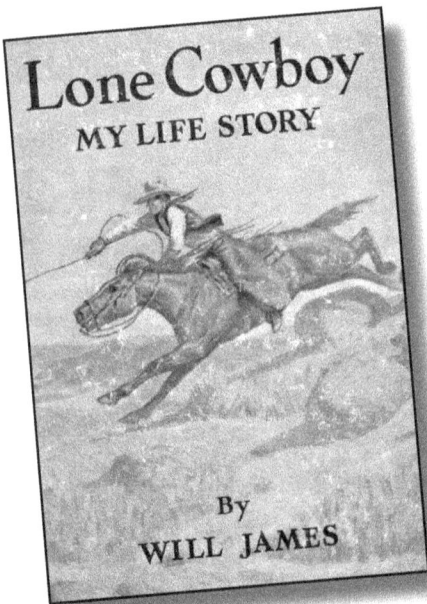

for an outfit, the brand is known." But in an introductory note to his readers, James justified the omission: "Here's a long story for you with no names in it to speak of—so you won't be bothered by the names of the creeks and cow camps you might never heard of, and of riders you wouldn't know."

Although James welcomed the praise that came with his books, handling the fame was difficult. In the course of publishing books, he attended frequent signings and parties. To make it through the social activities, James increased his alcohol consumption to the extent that he began to drink daily, even in his studio. Despite a growing addiction to alcohol, James continued an impressive output of writing and drawing. During the next decade he wrote fourteen books, including six novels and three children's books.

Although James made several attempts to overcome his alcoholism, he passed away from the disease on September 3, 1942, in Hollywood, California, at 50 years of age. Mourned by admirers from coast to coast, his ashes were spread near the Pryor Mountains in Montana with his saddle horses, Pecos and Cortez, grazing nearby.

Much was learned about Will James after his death. His first biographer, Anthony Amaral, discovered in the early 1960s that James had fabricated the early part of his life story. While doing research in the courthouse in Billings, Amaral found several depositions relating to the probate of James' last will and testament, which demonstrated that the Will James of *Lone Cowboy* fame was, in reality, Ernest Dufault, born in Ontario, Canada.

When James began writing his autobiography, he allegedly thought he wouldn't be taken seriously if he admitted to being born French-Canadian instead of on the Montana range. Consequently, he fabricated the early years of his life story. No matter where he was born or what his name was, however, Will James became America's quintessential cowboy, and the vitality and authenticity of his stories and drawings of the western range have never been equaled.

"The Nevada Mustang"

Frank Hoffman

"There's corral dust on his overalls, echoes of horseman's talk in his speech, the squint that comes from looking at far horizons under a blazing sun in his eye—and in his artist's hands the ability to recapture all the work, hardship, and joy of his far adventuring and put it on canvas for wall-bound men to see."

That's a description of Frank B. Hoffman, an early-day illustrator and rancher from Taos, as he was described in 1946 in a calendar promotion of his work by Brown and Bigelow. Hoffman was indeed a rancher who loved the land and his horses almost as much as he loved his art. But he might never have made his way to Taos, and the lifestyle it offered, had he not met the noted Russian artist Leon Gaspard at a one-man show at the Art Institute of Chicago in 1918.

Gaspard sung the praises of Taos in their conversations, and a year later Hoffman spent the summer painting with Gaspard in Taos—paying Gaspard $25 for each critique of his work. They painted and sketched outdoors all summer, often using the same models, including Gaspard's personal horses, some Indian ponies, and a few burros. Hoffman was so impressed with Gaspard's colorful palette and the loose style in which he painted that it was inevitable that his own work later reflected Gaspard's influence, particularly in his use of heavy pigment in an impressionistic manner.

Taos stood in sharp contrast to the bustling Chicago where Hoffman was born in 1888 and where he had been studying art and doing advertising and magazine illustrations. Instead, in Taos there were all sorts of saddle horses, wagons and teams, cowboys, Mexicans, and Indians for him to use as subjects. As others had before him, Hoffman found Taos and its mountains and deserts, clean dry air, and bright sun an ideal place to paint. For two summers he returned to paint with Gaspard, vowing to someday make Taos his home.

Hoffman's path to New Mexico was circuitous at best. Before his pivotal meeting with Gaspard he had worked at a variety of jobs: exercising horses on tracks in the South, Midwest, and Canada; swinging a sledge hammer ten hours a day, six days a week in a steel mill in Gary, Indiana; boxing in tournaments and even winning several Golden Glove bouts.

At a time when he was sorely disillusioned, he met Joseph E.J. Ryan, a family friend and editor of the *Chicago American Weekly*. Ryan saw some of Hoffman's horse drawings and thought enough of them that he told Hoffman about a job in his newspaper's art department. Although Hoffman had never considered drawing for a living, he decided that it was a much preferred occupation over boxing, even without pay until he proved he could draw.

Hoffman was sent with city reporters to make on-the-scene pencil sketches at such varied events as prize fights, jury trials, matinees, fires, and operas. Late into the night he worked his sketches into ink drawings, often using a brush instead of a pen, an idea he gleaned from studying Chinese lettering on advertisements he saw on streetcars as he rode to work. The technique reproduced well, and he was to use it extensively throughout his career.

Frank Hoffman in his Taos studio.

While at the newspaper, Hoffman was asked by Ray Long, editor of *Redbook*, to illustrate a dog story by James Oliver Curwood. Other assignments followed which boosted his confidence, but he still felt handicapped because he had not received formal training in oil painting, which magazine art editors required for story illustrators. For the next five years, he sandwiched art classes between newspaper assignments, studying with J. Wellington Reynolds at the Chicago Art Institute.

In the spring of 1916, having been rejected for military service in World War I due to a slight eye defect, Hoffman traveled to northern Montana where he had been hired by the Great Northern Railroad to paint wildlife to promote Glacier National Park. He painted elk, deer, buffalo, and moose in the mountains and on the nearby plains, often traveling horseback and leading a packhorse. He met and sketched many Indians, cowboys, miners, and other frontiersmen and used them for subject matter for the rest of his life.

In Montana he also became acquainted with John Singer Sargent, who was painting portraits of older members of the Blackfoot tribe on their reservation. He learned much from the hours he spent talking to Sargent and watching him paint, and the association inspired him to work harder on his own painting.

During the Taos summers of 1920-1921, Hoffman became friends with Walter Ufer and Herbert Dunton, who encouraged him to apply for membership in the Taos Society of Artists. Although flattered by their praise of his work, Hoffman felt he could not financially afford to paint solely for exhibition. Instead, he adopted a routine of spending summers in New Mexico painting for pleasure, and wintering in Chicago working on the increasing number of advertising commissions he was receiving.

Among his clients were Cream of Wheat, General Electric, and Montgomery Ward, whose ads illustrated by his paintings appeared in many popular magazines. The exposure led to many important short story assignments, and it also led to Hoffman's marriage. One of the models he hired for a Cream of Wheat commercial, Hazel Nelson, became his bride in May 1925. They spent that summer in Taos buying turquoise and silver jewelry, pottery, and saddle blankets from Indian traders, going to pueblos for dances, riding horseback in the mountains, watching rodeos, or completing painting projects scheduled for delivery that fall.

On their return to Chicago, Hoffman worked at a furious pace to complete a heavy load of advertising and magazine assignments. His output through the year that followed was phenomenal as evidenced by the number of times his work appeared in magazines during 1926. That spring his illustrations accompanied Zane Grey's serialized western, "Forlorn River," which was published in the *Ladies' Home Journal*. Before the year was over he had illustrated stories written by Peter B. Kyne, Mary Heaton Vorse, Lucia Zora, Florence Dorsey Welch, Guy Fletcher, and Zack Cartwright. The stories were published in the *Ladies' Home Journal, Liberty, Shrine, Country Gentleman, Cosmopolitan,* and *Woman's Home Companion*. In addition, five of his paintings appeared in full-page magazine ads.

Most of the stories were on western themes, although two dealt with horse racing and another two with prize fighting, both subjects about which Hoffman had personal knowledge. In this he differed from many of his contemporaries who frequently had to rely on book research to carry out their assignments. In describing his illustrations, Hoffman once said that they resulted from what he knew, what he saw, and what he felt. Moreover, his popularity with editors and writers stemmed from his ability to embellish a story with pictures instead of simply describing scenes he found within.

The majority of his story illustrations up to that time had been done for the *Ladies Home Journal*. Due to favorable reader response to his work, he was interviewed by the magazine's editors on their November 1926 "Our Family Album" page.

WILD HORSE MESA—By Zane Grey

When asked about his background and his talent in painting animals, especially horses, he replied, "I never said that I'd been a cowboy...but you can tell anyone that I sure like to draw a 'hawss.' A lot of folks figure that because I draw cowpunchers and cowponies, I am or have been a cowboy. That isn't true. I've knocked about different camps a lot, but that's all. I can rope my horse, and I've broken a few broncs, too. I reckon I've been thrown more times than the Prince of Wales. They'll tell you that in Taos. I own two of the

Turning a Stray

best cow ponies in New Mexico, two that have worked at their trade. The horses I draw and paint are what I call typical cow horses, and are big enough and strong enough to carry a man and hold a steer after he's down. It's a great country, the West. I love it. All I yearn for is a place on the side of a mountain—about 100 acres. That will do me for the rest of my life."

Two years later, in the fall of 1928, Hoffman found the place he was looking for. It was a sprawling adobe ranch house and 200 acres of sagebrush located two miles from the Taos Plaza. He named it Hobby Horse Rancho and, with the help of two Taos Indians, he created a studio there. Once the house was ready, his first project was a set of illustrations for "Desert Bloom," a Vingie Roe story that later appeared in the August 1929 issue of *McCall's*. The story was a western romance set in Arizona, and Hoffman's pictures were some of the best he had ever done for a magazine. They attested to the fact that he felt comfortable in his new home.

By 1931 Hoffman had painted dozens of oil paintings, either to illustrate short stories or magazine ads. His work had brought him financial security and a popular following among those who knew his work. But like so many illustrators, he was continually burdened with the stress of having to meet deadlines imposed by art editors. He was sometimes late with paintings, often because he scraped down canvases that were not to his satisfaction. He once said in defense of his work that "an artist should be judged by the best he produces. Especially...in judging work where delivery dates were often a deciding factor."

Consequently, at the end of 1931, he took a well-deserved break from illustrating. He and his wife had been training thoroughbreds at their ranch for several years and they decided to take six of their best two year-olds to the winter racing season in southern California. In spite of the fact that the colts developed colds and were unable to start any races, Hoffman returned to Taos charged with the idea of devoting his artistic efforts to painting art quality pictures of thoroughbreds, the horses that had been a part of his youth.

Over the next year he completed three paintings of his own horses that brought him immense satisfaction, primarily because he was painting for himself and not for art editors. While his paintings of thoroughbreds were exceptional, Hoffman was unable to attract commissions from interested owners to paint their horses. Several trips to Chicago and Long Island sparked interesting discussions about the idea, but he received no actual commissions.

While on Long Island Hoffman wrote his wife in Taos, explaining that his failure was due not only to the economic conditions of the Depression, but that there was "no tradition in America for the painting of horses, especially thoroughbreds," by artists trained in the traditional school of fine art. He further commented that tinted photographs seemed to satisfy most owners' need for pictures of their prized horses. Thus, Hoffman was forced to return to illustrating, where he knew that his services were in demand.

He worked first from the ranch in Taos, and then in a Chicago studio where he moved in 1937 to be closer to clients. In December 1939,

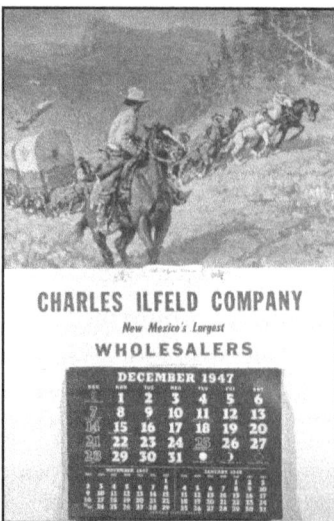

CHARLES ILFELD COMPANY
New Mexico's Largest
WHOLESALERS

DECEMBER 1947

at the age of 51, Hoffman conceived an idea as a new avenue for his work, one that eventually led to the most lucrative time of his career. Early in the month he wrote the Brown & Bigelow Company of St. Paul, Minnesota, requesting the opportunity to submit some western sketches for potential calendar pictures.

At that time Brown & Bigelow was the largest calendar house in the United States, whose devotion to high artistic standards clearly set them apart from their competitors. Norman Rockwell, Maxfield Parrish, Dick Bishop, and

R.H. Palenske were among the artists who painted for the company and helped it attain national prominence.

Some years earlier they had used paintings by Frederic Remington, Charles Russell, and other western artists for calendar illustrations, but at the time they did not offer a line of western subjects. Assuming they were familiar with his years as a western illustrator, Hoffman hoped he might interest them in his work. In 1942 Hoffman's "Trouble on the Trail" appeared as the first of more than 150 Brown & Bigelow calendar paintings that he would complete before failing eyesight forced him to give up painting.

He was given the latitude to determine the subject and situation depicted. Almost all of these paintings were characterized by rich colors and a strong human interest story-telling quality. A survey of the completed paintings reveals his familiarity with a wide variety of animals and confirms that he could paint—and liked to paint—more than just "a hawss." In both contemporary and historical portrayals he painted Indians or white hunters pursuing deer, elk, buffalo, moose, antelope, bighorn sheep, mountain lions, Canadian geese, ducks, quail, prairie chickens, and wild turkeys. His fishermen angled for salmon, trout, muskie, or small and large mouth bass.

Early in their association Brown & Bigelow asked him to submit sketches for a planned twelve-part mailing card series of outdoor hunters and fishermen pictured in the field. He accepted the assignment, pleased with the opportunity to develop paintings based on his own imagination and experience in the outdoors, and not on the dictates of a scene from a story. He was offered $200 per finished picture, which was substantially less than he received for magazine illustrations, but sufficient given the possibility for more work and future increases.

Working steadily, Hoffmana completed the series and the response was gratifying. Brown & Bigelow's vice president, Harry Huse, wrote that three of the paintings were worthy of being feature calendar subjects, and he asked for replacements. In addition, because the possibility existed that their competitors might contact Hoffman for paintings after the series appeared, Huse requested that he not enter into an agreement with another company without notifying him. He made

Day Herding

clear the importance to the company of having exclusive rights to Hoffman's work.

Huse also asked Hoffman for biographical material and photographs they might use in promoting the series. He wrote to Hoffman, "The story we have in mind...in this promotion is...of your prominence as an American illustrator, especially as an illustrator of outdoor life and action, the story of the wide range of your...actual participation in the type of activity which you have illustrated for us."

A typical promotion for calendars featuring Hoffman's paintings read:

> Frank Hoffman is America's premiere adventure artist. His knowledge of the great outdoors is unparalleled among modern painters, his skill is as great with a brush as it is with a rifle or a paddle. Wild turkeys in the mountains near his New Mexico ranch home are his favorite game, a corral is a good place to work, and an Indian is a mighty good critic of the scenes Hoffman paints exclusively for you through Brown & Bigelow.

His ranch work paintings were popular with cowboys due to their realistic action and accurate detail. The authenticity of clothing, saddles, and equipment received high marks from them, a fact important to Hoffman who knew how quick they were to point out inaccuracies found in art pertaining to their livelihood. Many cowboys collected his calendars and used them to decorate the walls of their bunkhouses and cow camps. Those collections can sometimes still be found where they were originally hung, appreciated equally as well by today's ranch cowboys.

Because Brown & Bigelow marketed their calendars nationwide, Hoffman gained exposure that exceeded even that of his magazine illustrations. The company kept many of the originals to decorate offices, returning the rest to Hoffman who sold them only when contacted by a collector whom he knew and liked.

The strain on his eyes from painting over the course of his long career caused Hoffman to put down his brushes for the last time in the fall of 1953. He spent the next four years with Mrs. Hoffman at race tracks in Phoenix and Raton where she trained many of their horses for a number of successful outings. Inevitably disappointed over the loss of his eyesight for painting, he still enjoyed those final years watching his horses train and race. Finally his health failed and he died at his beloved Hobby Horse Rancho on March 11, 1958. He was buried on the ranch between two juniper trees in a grave that faced the mountains to the north.

In spite of the popularity of his work during his lifetime, Hoffman received little scholarly attention primarily because the majority of his work was commissioned and not done for exhibition. As a result, little of it has found its way into museums or gallery collections. But perhaps that is what Frank Hoffman would have wished, for he never sought critical review, except from Leon Gaspard and John Singer Sargent. He was content to satisfy his clients, trusting that his work would afterward speak for itself.

Randy Steffen

Randy Steffen spent a lifetime illustrating men on horseback. The distinguished western artist and historian got his start as a boy drawing pictures of cowboys and American Indians in the margins of his schoolbooks. During a thirty-year career as a writer and artist, Steffen was acclaimed as an authority on the dress, saddles, weapons, and equipment of riders throughout world history and especially the American West.

In 1974 he received an American Airlines Award and a Bicentennial Award from the Dallas Bicentennial Commission for his efforts in preserving and promoting American history. His career was capped in 1976 when he earned the American Exemplar Award at a ceremony in Valley Forge, Pennsylvania.

Born and raised on a Texas ranch, Steffen was an adept horseman. He grew up working cattle horseback with his father and continued cowboying as a teenager on neighboring ranches to earn money. As with many ranch kids, he considered punching cows for a living after high school, but his father encouraged him to apply to the US Military Academy instead. Steffen was accepted, but later transferred to the US Naval Academy, where he studied engineering. He received a commission in the spring of 1940 and immediately sailed to Europe. He spent World War II as an undercover intelligence officer.

Upon returning from the war, Steffen served as a project engineer for the Naval Air Service, but resigned after a year because he'd had enough office work. Longing to be horseback, he loaded his saddle and headed west to see California and the West Coast.

Steffen made it as far as Boulder City, Nevada, when his trip halted because of a war-related illness. He was hospitalized for two months, but by the time he was released he'd decided he liked the Nevada desert. On a ranch he leased outside of Las Vegas, Steffen started breaking colts and trading horses. He also rekindled his passion for drawing and painting horses, and he sold many pieces in Las Vegas galleries.

Eventually the horseman bought forty acres in Knight County and started training polo mounts. He especially liked the place because there was "plenty of open space in all four directions" that he could use to put miles on his horses. Soon afterward, he took a job with the Nevada Parks and Wildlife Service to catch mustangs at a state game preserve headquartered at Indian Springs. Steffen relished the long days horseback.

Next he signed a contract with the National Park Service in the summer of 1947 to gather wild horses on Death Valley National Monument. With the help of an experienced mustanger, Tom Weaver, and a 16-year-old Piute Indian boy, Steffen built an oval catch pen from timbers that the three dragged from the mountains seven miles away. Once the pen was built, the cowboys caught, roped, and trapped 265 head of horses in five weeks. They gelded the stallions and broke a few to supplement their saddle strings. They sold the mares to a buyer in Las Vegas and ended their mustanging adventure with money in their pockets.

In early 1948 Steffen received his first assignment to illustrate an article for *The Western Horseman*, then headquartered in Reno, Nevada. The magazine's editor, Bob Denhardt, hired Steffen to illustrate a story titled "I Want Some Cold-Blood in My Cow Horse" which appeared in the March-April 1948

issue. In the same issue Denhardt officially welcomed Steffen to the magazine's "corral" as a new artist.

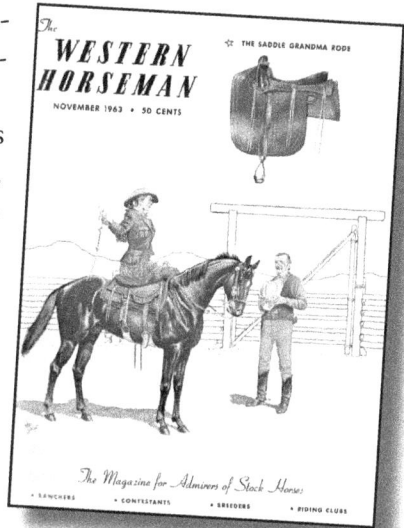

That year the magazine moved its editorial offices to Colorado Springs, Colorado. Denhardt persuaded Steffen to relocate too, so that he could assist Denhardt for six to eight months. Steffen's assignment was to design an office building for the magazine. Using drafting skills acquired at the US Naval Academy, the artist drew a set of plans for the building patterned after the Palace of the Governors located on the plaza in Santa Fe, New Mexico.

Having done his part to get the magazine up and running in its new location, Steffen moved to southern California where he rode polo ponies and got a few movie extra jobs. In 1950 he moved to his home state of Texas and edited a horse magazine that was in financial difficulty. The magazine folded after a few months, so Steffen decided to concentrate solely on writing about and drawing horses and horsemen. During 1952 he illustrated several *WH* articles, but he spent most of his time illustrating and writing the introduction to Ed Connell's significant work on the Californio horse tradition, *The Hackamore Reinsman*.

Steffen also contacted Dick Spencer, the new *WH* editor, about writing and illustrating various tips for horsemen, which first appeared in the January 1953 issue. Steffen contributed the tips under the titles *Hints for Horsemen, Horseman's Scrapbook,* and *Handy Hints,* and they eventually became a regular magazine section. Covering a broad spectrum of horse-related topics, Steffen developed some of them from his own experience and derived others from readers' ideas. He covered anything from fencing, trailering, training, and breeding to saddles, bits, and other horse equipment. His column became so popular that many readers turned first to find Steffen's tips before reading other parts of the magazine.

About the same time Steffen started contributing horseman's tips to *WH*, he was asked by another magazine to illustrate an article about a mounted US Cavalry soldier. When he began looking for research ma-

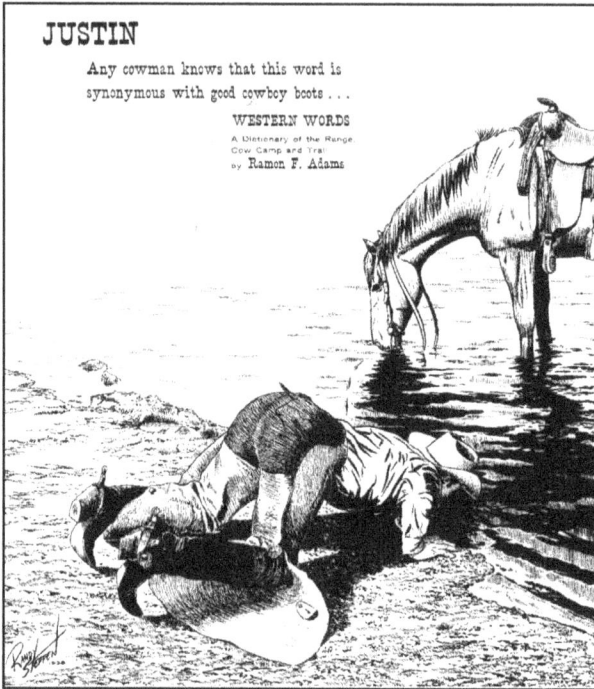

JUSTIN

Any cowman knows that this word is
synonymous with good cowboy boots . . .

WESTERN WORDS
A Dictionary of the Range,
Cow Camp and Trail
by Ramon F. Adams

terial for the drawings, he was surprised to find that there was so little published material on the subject. As a result, he promised himself to write and illustrate a book someday on cavalry uniforms, equipment, and horses. For the time being, though, he was forced to postpone the project in order to work on the articles and drawings that provided his income.

The articles he wrote and illustrated for *WH* pertained to a wide variety of horse-related subjects, but were mostly historical in nature. During the mid-1950s, Steffen devoted much of his time to an illustrated series of articles about horsemen from the historical past, ranging from the cavalry of Alexander the Great and Atila the Hun to the Comanche warriors and US cavalry of the 19th-century American West. In 1967 the articles were compiled into a *WH* book titled, *Horsemen Through Civilization* (now out of print).

Steffen had been born with a small hole in one of the chambers of his heart. As he grew older, the hole widened to the extent that in 1957 he underwent one of the earliest open-heart surgeries performed in the United States to repair the damage. The procedure was successful and allowed Steffen to continue to lead an active life, despite a weakened heart. An active life for Steffen meant pulling up stakes and moving back to California in 1958, where he finally devoted himself full-time to a book on the American cavalry. Two years later he bought a small ranch in the Sierra foothills and built a two-story log studio that enabled him to spread out his work and display the US military weapons, saddles, and uniforms he'd begun to collect.

As part of his research, he made trips to the Smithsonian Institution, Library of Congress, US Military Academy, and other eastern repositories to study military records and take photographs. In California he supplemented his writing income by working on the *Cisco Kid* television series. He either doubled for the series star, Duncan Rinaldo, or acted out fist fights with him.

By mid-1962 Steffen had completed the text and drawings for a cavalry book. He spent the fall preparing the material to send to a publisher, only to have tragedy strike on January 25, 1963. That morning Steffen left his ranch and returned in the afternoon to find that his studio had burned to the ground. Everything was lost, including his manuscript, collections, and ten years' worth of research notes, photographs, paintings, and drawings.

Despite the devastating loss, he regrouped and set out to replicate his work. Maintaining a positive attitude, he remarked to friends that, "At least this time I know where not to look," and he vowed to make his next effort even better. Two years later he moved to Florida to care for his aging parents, and he continued working feverishly on the cavalry project. Steffen still made time to write and illustrate for *WH*, and being on the East Coast made it easier for him to make the necessary research trips for his cavalry work.

In early 1971 Steffen once again returned to his native state of Texas. His health had begun to fail to the extent that his doctors told him it was too late for corrective heart surgery. They encouraged him to take as much strain off his heart as possible, and from that time on he was confined to a wheelchair.

His declining health created a great urgency to publish a horse-

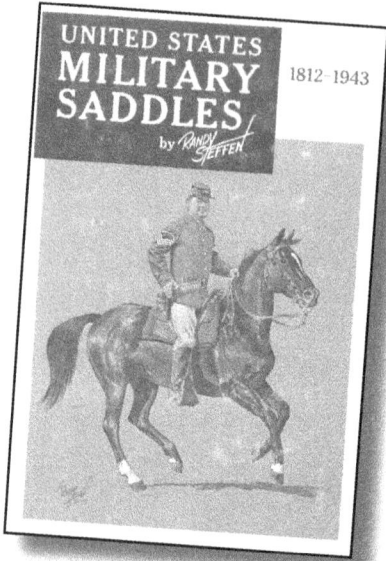

soldier book. He finished a second manuscript and a set of illustrations that he believed were not only more comprehensive than his first effort, but which would also serve as "a much more valuable source of reference." He sent the work to a publisher in New York who admired the thoroughness of the manuscript, but he rejected it because he felt it was too scholarly to be of reader interest.

Undaunted, Steffen sent the material to the University of Oklahoma Press, who had earlier shown an interest in the project. The press immediately agreed to publish it as a four-volume set, along with a volume devoted solely to US military saddles. While the books were in preparation, Steffen began sculpting in clay, a medium he had not worked with before. He demonstrated the same precision in conformation and detail that he previously exhibited in his paintings and drawings.

His book, *United States Military Saddles: 1812-1943*, was published in 1973. The publisher waited to reveal the first volume of his cavalry work, *The Horse Soldier: 1776-1943*, until 1977 to coincide with America's Bicentennial celebration. Horsemen, scholars, military enthusiasts, and museum curators alike praised the book. Steffen made clear in the preface to the first volume that his work wasn't another history of the United States Cavalry, but instead dealt with "the way the dragoons, the mounted rifleman, and the cavalryman looked; the weapons they fought with; and the saddles, bridles, and other horse gear they draped on their horses."

It was sad that Steffen never saw the published results of his monumental effort. He passed away on January 17, 1977, at the age of fifty-nine. His ashes were spread over one of his favorite places, the Wichita Mountains on the Kiowa and Comanche reservation in southwestern Oklahoma. Although he is no longer with us, Steffen's influence on preserving military history in print and his contributions to *WH* continue to live on and be remembered.

Lon Megargee

As a boy growing up in Philadelphia in the 1890s, Lon Megargee saw a performance of Buffalo Bill Cody's Wild West Show. Before the performance was over, he knew he wanted to be a cowboy.

Megargee showed little interest in school, so when his father died while the boy was still a teenager, he decided to follow his cowboy dream. He contacted some relatives who lived in Phoenix and asked if he could visit them. They readily agreed so he boarded a train and headed west.

The young man from the East assumed that because his relatives lived in Arizona they were ranchers. To his dismay, however, he found that his uncle was a dairy farmer. Nevertheless, he dutifully milked cows for a while, but soon bought a horse and saddle from a neighbor for ten dollars and left the farm without bothering to inform his uncle. His departure was slowed somewhat because he got bucked off three times before he got out of town.

His trail led toward Wickenburg where he got a job on the Bull Ranch. There he was befriended by Tex Singleton, known far and wide as a top hand, bronc rider, and two-gun man. Megargee learned the cowboy trade from Tex and exhibited a natural dexterity in handling a rope.

From the Wickenburg country, Megargee drifted to the Tonto Basin where he was hired at the Three Bars to ride broncs. After a time he returned to Phoenix and took a number of jobs ranging from night watchman, fire fighter, poker dealer to rope trick artist with Arizona Charlie's Wild West Show.

Anxious to return to the range, Megargee went north again and got a job riding broncs for Billy Cook's Double T outfit near New River. He eventually worked his way up to foreman of the ranch at the age of twenty-four.

With Billy Cook's help, Megargee put enough money together to buy five sections of range land. He named it El Rancho Cinco Uno and stocked it with six hundred mother cows. But as luck would have it for the aspiring rancher, he didn't get rain on the ranch for three years.

Megargee did everything he could to save his herd, from feeding cottonwood branches to the cattle to killing calves to save their mothers. But the drought eventually beat him. When his horses started eating loco weed, he knew it was time to call it quits and he reluctantly left the ranch for Phoenix.

Over the years Megargee had always enjoyed drawing. On the ranches where he worked he frequently sketched pictures of horses and cowboys on the backs of envelopes or whatever kind of paper he could find. Deciding to develop his talent, Megargee left Arizona for California where he enrolled in the Los Angeles School of Art and Design. He studied there for six months and concentrated on pencil drawing. He went back to Arizona when he felt he had learned all that he could.

A chance meeting with Arizona Governor George Hunt resulted in Megargee being able to concentrate on art. Hunt was a rancher and sympathized with the young man's ranching misfortune. Consequently, he urged Megargee to summit sketches for some murals of Arizona scenes that the state planned to use to decorate its new capitol building.

Several of his drawings were selected, and the money Megargee received from painting the murals allowed him to pursue art full time. He started working in oils, painting primarily ranch scenes and portraits of Arizona natives. He spent a lot of time traveling throughout the state looking for subject matter, especially in the north among the Navajo and Hopi Indians.

Before long he started receiving commissions to do the covers of several western magazines along with story illustrations. He also did some wall paintings of western scenes for the famous Porter's Saddle Shop in Tucson, as well as several paintings that were hung in homes in the Phoenix area.

Over his long career, his most famous painting was commissioned by the Stetson Hat Company in the early 1920s. Titled "Last Drop from His Stetson," the painting has been used by the company since that time as the most prominent image in its advertising campaigns. For more than seventy years, everyone who has worn a Stetson has seen Megargee's painting because every time they put their hat on they see it printed on the inside satin lining.

Megargee also painted some well known pictures for the Arizona Brewing Company headquartered in Phoenix. To promote the company's popular A-1 Beer, Megargee did a series of five pictures beginning in 1948. The first, "The Cowboy's Dream," was easily the most popular with cowpunchers. It depicted a cowboy asleep on his back using his saddle as a pillow. The clouds in the upper right form an undressed

woman riding a horse branded with A-1. Prints of the painting can still be found hanging in saloons and bars throughout the West.

In each succeeding year Megargee painted "Black Bart (The Barber and The Bandit)," "The Dude Lady," "The Quartet (Poker Flats)," and "Margarita." Because the pictures were so widely displayed, many people are familiar with them even though they have little idea who created them.

In 1933 Megargee built a sprawling adobe house and studio on six acres of land in Paradise Valley, a mile east of the Arizona Biltmore. He called it Casa Hermosa. There, in the shadow of Camelback Mountain he spent ten years painting and entertaining his many friends. Unfortunately, he was forced to sell his beloved home in the early 1940s because of financial difficulties encountered as a result of divorce. Nevertheless, he continued to paint the cowpunchers, Indians, and sunsets of his adopted state until his death in January of 1960.

Justin Wells

When Justin Wells was a school kid in Oklahoma in the 1950s, he amused himself by drawing pictures in the margins of his books when class didn't interest him. He drew mostly horses, which he knew a lot about because both his grandfather and father were horse breeders. Justin said the most memorable thing that happened to him growing up was when his dad decided he was old enough, at the age of eleven, to start his own colt.

Justin called the colt, a sorrel filly with a flaxen mane and tail, *Chico Rose*. After he broke her, he sold her for $1,000. She was the first of many that he later broke for his family and neighbors during his high school and college years. "I always had plenty of colts to ride—all I wanted," he said.

Consequently that meant Justin had plenty of them to draw and paint too. About horses Justin said, "I've always loved the way they look, either standing still or moving. They're works of art in themselves. For centuries they've been bred for a certain conformation, color, or size, which for me essentially makes them genetic sculptures."

"I had two brothers and growing up we all liked to draw. At

night around the kitchen table we'd challenge each other to draw an Indian or a cowboy on a horse, and then we'd start bragging about which drawing was the best. Our dad would judge the results, and he was good for us because he was a stickler for accurate conformation. He never failed to point out our mistakes and have us correct them."

"We'd either draw broncs out in the corral or copy photographs from western magazines or drawings from comic books. And, of course, we tried our hand at drawing Roy Rogers and Gene Autry and whoever else was in the movies or on television."

In 1975 Justin moved to Amarillo in the Texas Panhandle and opened a studio and gallery next door to Bob Marrs' saddle shop on Third Street. Marrs was one of the most popular saddle makers in the Panhandle at the time, and he attracted a lot of people to his shop located across from the livestock auction. When Marrs retired in 1993, Justin expanded into his shop so that he would have room not only to display his own work, but also his considerable collection of saddles, spurs, bridles, and other cowboy equipment.

As a result of being Bob Marrs' next door neighbor, Justin met and became friends with ranchers and cowboys from all over West Texas, Oklahoma, and eastern New Mexico who came into his gallery after they had gone to see Marrs. They started to invite him to help them during their spring and fall works, which he appreciated not only for the chance to get horseback, but for the opportunity to get ideas for paintings and drawings as well. The timing was perfect because by this time he had decided to devote his artistic efforts to capturing contemporary cowboy and ranch life.

Whether he was riding with the cowboys or simply taking photographs, he always delighted in noticing the changing styles of cowboys' clothing and equipment. "Over the years I've seen hat brims get wide and cantles get high just like they were once before. Probably the only thing that ever shocked me was the first time I saw a cowpuncher wearing a pair of chinks. I thought they were some kind of skirt," he once said with a twinkle in his eye.

"I moved to the Panhandle because I wanted to be in big ranch country where the ranches still run wagons, rope horses out of remudas, and drag calves to the fire like they did a hundred years ago. It's also the country of Charles Goodnight, Billy the Kid, and Charlie Siringo. You can still go to some of the places they went and see what they saw. Nothing much has changed. From the first time I saw it I always loved the short grass, flat top mesa country of the Panhandle. You can see into the middle of next week."

Furthermore he said, "Cattle people have always been a unique class of human being. They are distinctively recognizable apart from any other group of men who make their living outdoors, and they're some of the best people in the world. Besides, I always like visiting those ranches for the chance to eat their cooking."

After each trip he'd come home with plenty of ideas for pictures—anything from a branding scene, to cowboys doctoring cattle, or the remuda standing with their necks stretched over a rope corral waiting to be caught for the morning's work. "It seems that for every picture I did, an idea for ten more popped into my head. I've never run out of projects."

While still in Oklahoma, Justin had gained enough notoriety with his art that he began to be asked by various book and magazine editors to illustrate for them. His first paid illustration was for *Oklahoma Cattleman* in 1960. Since then he carried out hundreds of pictures for magazines such as *Cowboy Magazine, Western Horseman,* and *Quarter Horse Journal.* In addition he illustrated many books, probably the most well known being Jean Cates and Sue Cunningham's series of

131

chuckwagon cookbooks.

Both writers and editors like his work because, in the best tradition of illustrating, he has the ability to embellish a story with his pictures instead of simply describing scenes found within. Darrell Arnold, the editor and publisher of *Cowboy Magazine* used Justin for years to illustrate stories in his magazine. He commented that he liked that Justin didn't need photographs or other graphic aids to create his drawings. Furthermore, he said "You could lock him in a room with only a table, a chair, a pad, a pencil, and his talent and he'd come out with an accurate, realistic, and interesting cowboy drawing. He was a true student of the West and could draw or paint cowboys, horses, and western action as well as it can be done."

Justin's peers in the western art world also praised his work, not only from the technical aspect but because of its accuracy as well. New Mexico sculptor Curtis Fort remarked that, "Cowboys like Justin's pictures because they can tell in a second that he's been there. Nothing's ever out of place, whether it's a throat latch or a latigo. He's a lot different in that way than those artists that can sure draw and paint but don't know much about what they're drawing or painting. And the people that don't know anything about cowboy life can learn a lot about it just from looking at one of his pictures."

Some of Justin's paintings of cowboys and horses also appeared in a rather unusual format. In the 1990s a non-profit organization in

Amarillo came up with the idea of having local artists decorate life-size fiberglass horses, the proceeds from the sale of which were then contributed to various charitable organizations in the community. Justin painted seven of the horses and said he relished the challenge of doing a picture on something besides canvas or paper.

His studio art has also been used in a number of compilations of cowboy art including a woodcut of a chuckwagon that appeared in *The Cowboy in American Prints* by John Meigs and a number of paintings included in *The Texas Cowboy* published by Texas Christian University Press to celebrate the state's sesquicentennial in 1986.

Like his father and grandfather before him back in Oklahoma, Justin has raised colts since he moved to Amarillo. Working with them was the great joy of his life. "I have always found that riding has helped my art because knowing how a horse operates from personal experience, as opposed to simple observation, made it possible for me to communicate reality much more effectively, no matter what the scene may be."

During the last years of his life you could generally find Justin in one of three places. If not painting or sketching in his studio, he was probably out with his horses. And if not there you could be pretty sure he'd be at his favorite table at the livestock auction café discussing

cows and horses with friends. And sometimes he might even have been talking about drawing them.

On the afternoon of February 29, 2008, Justin came home from spending time with his horses to find his studio engulfed in flames and surrounded by four fire engines and thirty firefighters. He watched in disbelief as more than forty years of work plus his cowboy collections turn to ash before his eyes.

Afterward, he was philosophical about the devastating loss. Irrepressible as ever and showing the indomitable spirit he was known for, he remarked, "Some people say now and then a town needs a good fire so they can tear out all the junk and start all over. I guess I'll just do the same and start all over."

His friends and loyal collectors rushed to his aid and soon set him up with living quarters and studio space complete with art supplies. Before long he was drawing and painting again. But, in spite of putting up a good front, he confided in friends that the fire and the destruction of his things had hit him hard.

The physical toll was also considerable. So much so that Justin suffered a heart attack on June 15, 2008, that took his life at the age of sixty-seven. He was buried in a small cemetery near his home town in Oklahoma before a host of loyal friends, cowboys, ranchers, and collectors who all remembered how well he kept cowboy life alive through his pictures.

S. Omar Barker, the Cowboy's Poet

S. Omar Barker once described himself as the "cowboy's poet, not a cowboy poet." In a career that extended over seventy years, Barker wrote hundreds of short stories and factual articles about cowboy life and the outdoors. He is best remembered, however, for his poems, written with wit and understanding, about the habits, likes, and dislikes of the riding men he grew up with. Considered as a whole, everything he wrote was true to the range.

Omar Barker was born in 1894 on his parents' homestead in the mountains west of Las Vegas, New Mexico, the youngest of eleven children. His father was engaged in "farming, sawmilling, preaching, and running about a hundred head of cattle." Although Omar grew up doing his share of the cow work on the ranch, he later claimed the experience never made him a cowboy. He said he had been as familiar with pitchforks, plows, garden hoes, crosscut saws, axes, rifles, and fishing rods as he ever was with horses and saddles. Nevertheless, he decided early on that his true calling was to write about the range men whom he came to know and admire. His first attempt at writing resulted in a story about his family's ranch that was published in a farming magazine. He was twelve years old at the time, and for his effort he received the princely sum of $2.00 in the form of one hundred

two-cent stamps. Nevertheless, that was sufficient encouragement and he continued writing for the rest of his life.

After high school, Omar moved from the ranch to Las Vegas and entered New Mexico Normal University where he received a degree in education in 1922. For the next few years he taught English in several small-town New Mexico schools, although he continued to write whenever he found time.

As a diversion, he next spent a year as a Forest Ranger, and then bought some cows that he pastured in the same mountain valley where he grew up. He later described his ranching by saying, tongue-in-cheek, "At one time I owned a few droop-horned cows and a spotted mule. When I applied for registration of a Lazy SOB as my brand, I was told that some other S.O.B. already had it."

By the end of the decade Barker decided he had sufficient success in getting his work published that he put everything else aside and began to write full-time. Late in life he estimated that during his career he had written and published more than two thousand poems, or verses as he called them, fifteen hundred fiction stories, and twelve hundred non-fiction articles. All of them dealt with the Southwest in some way or another, although most were about cows, cowboys, or horses.

His writings appeared in magazines and periodicals both great and small, and as varied as *Saturday Evening Post, Field and Stream*, the *Wall Street Journal,* and the *New York Times*. The long list of western magazines that he contributed to, most of which are no longer in existence, included *Western Story Magazine, Ranch Romances, Thrilling Ranch Stories, Wild West Weekly, Two-Gun Western Magazine, Ace High, Hoofs*

Omar and Elsa Barker

and Horns, Western Rangers, Cowboy Stories,* and *Rangeland Stories* among many others. His best known poem by far is "A Cowboy's Christmas Prayer" which first appeared in *Ranch Romances*, but was later reprinted more than one hundred times. It was even distributed in Braille.

In 1928 he compiled a number of his published western poems into a book

titled *Buckaroo Ballads*. That was followed
by another compilation, *Songs of the Sad-
dlemen*, in 1954 and *Rhymes of the Ranges*
in 1968. Fortunately for the present gen-
eration of western readers, a collection of
Barker's poems was compiled under the
title, *Cowboy Poetry, Classic Rhymes by S.
Omar Barker*, in 1998.

Barker was once notified that a twelve-
year-old boy and aspiring cowpuncher
had selected one of his poems to recite
in an interscholastic competition. The
boy's English teacher, however, would
not allow him to use the poem until the un-
grammatical cowboy lingo had been corrected. The boy stuck to his
guns and refused to enter the contest if he could not use Barker's poem
as written.

Omar wrote the boy a consoling letter, apologizing to him that the
poem did not fit the teacher's standards. But he explained that, "a basic
principle of professional authorship is to write true to the life of the
kind of people we are writing about. We do not make cowboys talk like
professors of English but like cowboys."

"I believe that learning correct English is an important part of education; but don't let it get you down that your teacher apparently disap-
proved of the cowboy lingo in my poem. I was raised on a ranch among
men who talked that way, and I'm still not ashamed of their kind of
talk."

"On the other hand, honest-to-god cowfolks are the people I most
respect and admire, and I am proud to be able to talk their language,
whether correct grammatically or not."

"A good, all around education is mighty important, but so is knowing about horses and cattle outside of books. There is no finer or more
useful life than ranching, and I wish you well in your ambition to follow that road."

Omar Barker passed away in 1985 at his home in Las Vegas, but
his poems have not been forgotten. As with the work of Badger Clark,
Bruce Kiskaddon, Curley Fletcher, or Henry Herbert Knibbs, a lot of
contemporary cowboy poets are fond of reciting Barker's poems not
only because of their authenticity, but their humor as well. Invariably,

one or two of Omar's verses are recited at each of the various cowboy poetry gatherings held across the West today.

In the same manner, his poems are still popular with cowboys on ranches throughout the West. As they have for years, cowpunchers can still be found reciting Barker favorites to friends, whether it be in the bunkhouse and at the tail end of a cow drive.

~~~~~~~~~~~~~~~~~~~~~~~

Cowboy Lore from S. Omar Barker

On shoeing horses --

Of all the ol' back-achin' jobs a cowpokes's got to do,
There's mighty few as tough as when he's got a bronc to shoe...
Some ponies are such leaners, that I've heard ol' cowboys say
That once they've had to shoe 'em, they can tell you what they weigh.

But if the horse gets wringy, and they bang a careless thumb,
There ain't much doubt but what you'll hear the cowpokes cussin' some,
For tackin' on the horse shoes, just to tell it fair and square
cain't never be done proper if you ain't learned how to swear!

from "Tackin' on the Shoes"

On boots --

The cowboy is as proud a cuss as every you will meet.
And specially fastidious about his dainty feet.
He figgers that they wasn't made to walk upon a heap,
Like those of men that wield a spade or heard a bunch of sheep.
That's maybe why the high-heeled boot he wears at work or play
Sometimes will cost this proud galoot purt near a whole month's pay.
He'll short himself on trips to town and pass up payday pleasure
To lay a wad of money down for new boots made-to-measure.

from "Boot Galoot"

On cow horses and breaking broncs --

There's different ways for tamin' broncs to be good saddle hosses,
And every colt has got to learn to savvy who the boss is;
But lots of cowhands tell me that the best hoss, in the end,
Is one some good horsebreaker always treated like a friend.

from "Breakin' the Broncs"

Of all God's creatures I endorse
Most heartily the one called "horse."
That on this creature man might sit
No doubt is why God made him split!

from "Cowboy's Opinion"

His pride in his rough callin'
Don't require much caterwaulin' –
He's the most unbraggin' cuss you'll come across;
But you mighty sure can figger
That no brag is ever bigger
Than a cowboy's when he's braggin's on his hoss!

from "Buckaroo Braggin'"

When a bronco gives way to man-throwin' itch,
In Texas they say that he lets in to "pitch,"
While up in Wyoming, as no doubt you've heard,
Them salty bronc peelers claim "buck" is the word.

Now this is a point you can argue, my friend,
Till the last rope is raveled plum out to the end;
But all hands agree that when broncos explode,
It ain't what you call it that gits a man throwed!

from "The Word Don't Matter"

On punching cows --

Most cowpokes will tell you that here is a truth
You might as well learn in the days of your youth:
To be a cowpuncher you'll never learn how
Unless you are purt near as smart as the cow!

from "Texas Truth"

On saddling and saddles --

They asked me why a cowboy saddles up with quiet care.
It's partly just a cowboy trait to treat his pony fair.
He may not ever pet him much, nor pamper him, nor sugar him.
But if a hoss is fit to ride, it don't make sense to booger him.

from "Saddlin' Up"

There's one thing I've noticed that galls his inside.
It's a lotta stuff tied on the saddle he rides:
For the "hired man a-horseback," from head down to feet,
Sure dotes on a riggin' that's trim and that's neat.

from "Cowboy Likin's"

They asked me "What's a saddle?" So I told 'em it's a kack,
A rig of wood and leather shaped to fit a horse's back.
You set up in its middle with a leg hung down each side,
Some horse meat in between 'em, and that is known as ride.

from "Pants Polisher"

On roping hard and fast --

For them ol' tie-fast cowboys, Here is a rule that fits:
Whatever you get your rope on, It's yours - or else you're its!

from "Rule of the Range"

On hats --

With cowboys - and women - it works out like that:
Their spirits pick up when they wear a new hat!

from "Sombrero"

On neck rags –

It might be silk or it might be cotton –
The ol' bandana won't be forgotten.
Around his neck everywhere he went,
Twas a sure 'nough cowboy implement...

It might be red or it might be blue,
And often some kind of a faded hue,
But a cowboy without it, out in the West,
Considered himself just about half-dressed!

from "The Ol' Bandana"

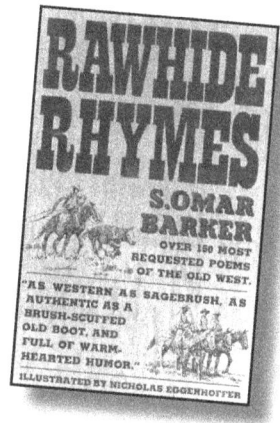

RAWHIDE RHYMES
S. OMAR BARKER
OVER 150 MOST REQUESTED POEMS OF THE OLD WEST.
"AS WESTERN AS SAGEBRUSH, AS AUTHENTIC AS A BRUSH-SCUFFED OLD BOOT, AND FULL OF WARM-HEARTED HUMOR."
ILLUSTRATED BY NICHOLAS EGGENHOFFER

Will Rogers and His Horses

From the time Will Rogers was a boy, he had two consuming interests—horses and roping. Throughout a celebrated career on stage, radio, in movies and Wild West Shows, America's most loved cowboy always had horses, no matter where his trail took him. Of the dozens of horses he owned and rode over his lifetime, Comanche, Teddy, Dopey, and Soapsuds stood out as his favorites.

Will was born on the Cherokee Indian reservation near Oologah in northeastern Indian Territory on November 4, 1879. Like ranch kids everywhere, he rode from an early age, most often with a rope in his hand. One story is that at age six he roped a neighbor's turkey whose neck broke as it tried to get away. After admitting the deed to the bird's owner and promising not to commit the transgression again, the boy unashamedly remarked that, in spite of what he had done, he would stay until the bird was ready for dinner.

Although Will had his pick of horses, his favorite was a dun called Comanche that his father gave him when he was ten years old. The horse was five years old at the time and stood 14 hands high. Will later wrote that Comanche was so fast he could "put you so close to a steer that you didn't rope him, you just reached over and put a 'hackamore' on him."

When Will was thirteen his father took him to see Buffalo Bill's Wild West Show at

141

the Chicago World's Fair. Although he enjoyed watching the hard riding cowboys and Indians, he was most impressed with the Mexican
rope artist, Vincente Cropeza. When he returned home, he began du-
plicating as many of the roper's tricks as he could.

Will attended several schools as a young man but seemed more interested in roping steers than studying books. His father believed he
required more discipline, so he enrolled his son at Kemper Military
Academy in Missouri when he was seventeen. Always the cowboy, Will
arrived for admission dressed in a red shirt and bandana with his pants
tucked inside his red-topped boots. His lariat ropes were coiled around
his suitcase.

Not surprisingly, the regimentation of military school did not suit
him. After a year he quit and left for Texas to punch cows. He traveled
by train to Higgins, Texas, and got a job on the Little Robe Ranch east
of town. After helping the ranch brand in the spring, he went with a
trail herd to Kansas and then rode to Amarillo where he got another
job trailing steers.

Afterward he went to California with a trainload of cattle but soon
got homesick and decided to return home. There his father bought him
a herd of cattle, but Will spent more time in contests roping steers and
riding broncs than tending to the ranch.

On the fourth of July 1899, he won first place at a roping competition in Claremore, Indian Territory, and then took his horse Comanche
by train to St. Louis to perform in Colonel Zack Mulhall's Wild West
Show. Afterward he toured with Mulhall's cowboy band that played
at shows throughout the Midwest. Although Will did not play an in-
strument, he pretended to play a trombone at each performance until
Mulhall called him out of the stands to ride a bronc or rope a steer.

Will became progressively bored with life on the ranch, feeling that
it was tame compared to punching cows in Texas, going to ropings, or
performing in Wild West Shows. At that time there was talk among his
friends about Argentina, where there were still big ranches and wide
open country. Will decided to see for himself. His father was reluctant
to let him go at first but later agreed and bought his son's cattle so he
would have money to travel.

Before Will left he went to see Jim Rider, a friend who had a carved
California saddle that Will liked. He asked Rider to sell it to him and
after much negotiation, Rider traded his saddle not only for Will's
saddle, but for several Navajo saddle blankets and fifty dollars as well.

Packing his new saddle, Will left with Dick Parris and traveled to New Orleans, then sailed to New York, London, and finally Buenos Aires. They toured the country but were disillusioned with what they saw. In a letter to his father Will wrote that "the work and cattle business here is nothing like it is at home...They drive the cattle in a run... In cutting out there are from two to three men to each animal. They would not begin to believe that a horse knew enough to cut out a cow without guiding."

He found that there were few Americans working cattle in Argentina after all, and in a patriotic vein he wrote that "as for roping and riding, [the Argentines] can't teach the punchers in America anything." He proudly remarked that "my saddle and all have been a big show ever since they seen it." Always concerned about his horses, he asked his father to "please see that they take care of my ponies and don't let anyone use them. Papa, don't let old Comanche be touched till I come home."

His companion Dick Parris decided to return home, and Will paid his passage which left him broke. He had to leave his hotel and live off money he earned roping mules until he heard of a job tending stock on a ship headed for South Africa. Although he was not enthusiastic about feeding cattle, horses, and mules on a boat for two months, he hired on thinking it was a way to get back to the United States. When the ship arrived in South Africa, he helped drive the stock to a farm two hundred miles away where he stayed and worked for two months.

He then took a train to the coast, only to find when he arrived that his prized saddle had been stolen. Undeterred, he got a job driving mules with some natives to the town of Ladysmith two hundred and fifty miles away. There he met a man by the name of Texas Jack who owned a Wild West show then touring the country. When the show-man discovered that Will could rope, he gave him a job, billing him as "The Cherokee Kid, The Champion Lasso Thrower of the World" and paying him twenty dollars a week.

Will wrote his father that he "was hired to do roping in the ring, but the man who rides the pitching horses is laid off and I have been riding [for him] ever since I have been with the show...I have learned to do quite a bit of fancy roping, and it takes fine over here where they know nothing whatever about it."

The problem with being a trick roper in South Africa, however, was the difficulty in obtaining suitable ropes. In a letter dated March 27, 1903, Will wrote his father asking him to send him "some rope. I want 100 feet of the best kind of hard twist rope. You can get it there. Any of the boys will show you what I used to use. Pretty small, but hard twist. I can't get a thing here that we use. Some nights I rope with old tie ropes or any old thing."

Will spent nine months with Texas Jack, and they became close friends. He later said it was one of the most important friendships of his life because of what Jack taught him about showmanship and performing before an audience. He assured his father that life in the show was reputable because "Jack don't drink a drop or smoke or gamble and likes his men to be the same."

Nevertheless, Will still wanted to go home. He heard about a Wild West Circus touring Australia, so he left Texas Jack and sailed to Australia hoping to soon get back to the United States. After touring Australia and New Zealand for several months, he had enough money to book passage to San Francisco.

Back in Indian Territory, he joined Colonel Mulhall's Wild West Show at the St. Louis World's Fair in the summer of 1904. When the engagement was over, Will acted on a suggestion Texas Jack had given him and worked up a roping act to perform on the vaudeville stage. He traveled to Chicago and got work in several theaters. He soon decided to expand his act by adding horse catches because at the time no one had ever roped a running horse on stage.

Will knew that Colonel Mulhall's wife in Indian Territory had the perfect horse for the act, so he took a train to their ranch and bought him for $100. He named him Teddy after President Roosevelt and began training him for a routine on stage.

In April of the next year Will shipped Teddy and Comanche to New York to perform with Colonel Mulhall's show at Madison Square Garden. During one performance a steer jumped out of the arena and ran loose among the audience scattering them in panic. Will followed the steer and roped him which brought cheers from the crowd. The next morning an account of his heroics appeared on the front page of the New York Times.

Will's purpose for going to New York was to put his act with Teddy on stage. Consequently, he left Mulhall and made his New York stage debut on June 11, 1905. Wearing either a red or blue flannel shirt, chaps, and a small Stetson hat, he began his act by riding Teddy on stage and performing several tricks in the saddle. Afterward, he stepped off and gave the horse an affectionate pat on the rump to send him off.

He next did a series of solo tricks and then called for Teddy who was ridden by Buck McKee. On cue the horse dashed on stage, and Will caught him by four feet. On the next pass, Will threw two ropes catching Buck with one and Teddy with the other.

One newspaper called Will the "King of the Lariat," and reported that "with the horse and rider traveling across the stage, [he] caught [Teddy] about the neck by throwing the lasso with his foot. One of the most interesting feats was shown when the horse and rider were on one end of the stage, and Rogers standing at the other twirled the rope in such a way that he put a double noose about the man's wrists, then he bound the wrists to the saddle (horn) and put nooses about the horse's neck and nose without approaching it. His last feat was letting out a lasso eighty-two feet long and swinging it about his head while on horseback."

Before he started his act in New York, Will sold Comanche. He explained to his sister that, "I sold old Comanche to a man in New York, and Mulhall sneakingly bought him from him for little Mildred (Mulhall's daughter). He bought him when he found out I was going to stay east...He thought I would follow him as he was mad because I quit."

A few years later Mulhall told Will that Comanche was never used in the show, but was instead turned out in a pasture in Florida. When told of Comanche's whereabouts, Will made plans to ship him home, but his old friend died before he could get it done.

For several years Will had carried on a relationship with a girl from home by the name of Betty Blake. Theirs was an on-again, off-again relationship due primarily to Will's career in show business, but in 1908 she finally accepted his proposal of marriage. They married in November and moved to a house on Long Island that had stables for Will's horses.

Will, Buck, and Teddy performed in cities all over the East and in Europe until 1910 when Will decided to retire Teddy because of the expense of travel. He shipped him home and had him turned out on the ranch. Some time later Teddy turned up missing and was not located for several months when he was found pulling a plow for one of Will's fellow Cherokee tribesmen. The erstwhile equine star was brought back to the ranch where he placidly lived out the rest of his life.

Will and Betty Rogers had three children while living in New York; Will, Jr., born October 1911; Mary, born May 1913; and Jim, born July 1915. The month Jimmy was born, Will bought a round-bodied black horse with glass eyes that he called Dopey. He described the horse as being "the gentlest and greatest pony for grownups or children anyone ever saw. I don't know why we called him Dopey. I guess it was because he was always so gentle and just the least bit lazy. Anyhow, we meant no disrespect to him."

"He helped raise the children. During his lifetime he never did a wrong thing to throw one of them off, or a wrong thing after they had fallen off. He couldent pick 'em up, but he would stand there and look at 'em with a disgusted look for being so clumsy as to fall off. I used to sit on him by the hour and try new rope tricks, and he never batted an eye."

While living on Long Island, Will learned to play polo, a natural game for him because it required riding a horse. He was taught by a cowboy friend from Texas, Jim Minnick, who was in New York training polo ponies. When Will first started playing, he rode his roping horses, his favorite being Bootlegger who, although undersized, was fast and agile. Later he bought a string of trained polo mounts.

After playing the game for some time and learning how strenuous it was on both horse and rider, Will said that "the people that think riding a horse is all there is to polo are the same people who think that anybody that can walk makes a good golfer or anybody who looks good in a bathing suit makes a good swimmer...They call it a gentleman's game for the same reason that they call a tall man, 'Shorty.'"

In the early years of performing on stage Will rarely spoke to his audience. Later he began making natural, off-the-cuff remarks either about other performers or the rope tricks he was doing. When he found that his observations made the audience laugh, he incorporated them as a part of his routine.

For example, after completing a particularly difficult trick he would say, "Worked that pretty good, made my joke and trick come out even." However, when a trick did not go well, he remarked that "I've only got jokes enough for one miss. I've either got to practice roping or learn more jokes." One of his favorite quips was to tell the audience that "swinging a rope is all right when your neck ain't in it."

In 1915 Florence Ziegfield hired Will to rope in between dance productions of his Ziegfield Follies show and substantially increased his salary. Will performed two shows a day and added home-spun commentary about national affairs that he gathered from the newspapers he read each day.

Because of Will's notoriety with the Follies, film maker Samuel Goldwyn hired him to make movies in California in 1918. Will and

Betty moved there the following year and bought a house in Beverly Hills, adding a stable, barn, and riding ring in the back. Will planted so many trees around the house that he quipped, "You could conduct a real nice hanging in my front yard."

Will appeared in a dozen silent pictures, often doing his own stunt riding on a horse he owned named Chapel. Afterward, he produced three films of his own, the most notable being *A Roping Fool,* which showcased the tricks he performed on stage. Dopey starred in the equine role doing what Teddy had done previously. Will used white ropes and filmed many of the tricks in slow motion so that the audience could better follow them. When the film was finished, he stated that "I don't think you [can] consider it art, but there is thirty years of hard practice in it."

Afterward, Will went back to the Follies. He was also in demand as an after-dinner speaker, and that allowed him to expand on the political and social commentary of his Follies act. In addition, he began writing a newspaper column for the *New York Times* titled, "Will Rogers Says," which was later syndicated to papers all over the United States.

In the spring of 1925 Will bought ranch land in the Santa Monica Mountains west of Los Angeles and built a headquarters complete with a house, stables, roping corral, and polo field. He cut trails in the mountains so he and his family and friends could ride through them, and he put in a four-hole golf course for his guests. Even though he did not play himself, he enjoyed following the players around horseback explaining that "I'd play golf if a fellow could [do] it on a horse."

The ranch was Will's refuge when he was not making movies or traveling. Betty wrote that every time he came home, he spent time horseback, either roping calves, playing polo, or riding mountain trails. "I think he would have been satisfied to spend his entire life astride a horse," she said. "He used to say, 'There is something the matter with a man who don't like a horse.'" Of all his diversions on the ranch, he probably enjoyed roping calves the most. He rarely

saddled a horse without tying a rope to the horn, and
he always had fresh calves to
turn into the roping corral. He
even practiced indoors where
he had a stuffed calf mounted
on wheels. He once remarked
tongue-in-cheek that he was
"the best dead-calf roper in the
world, but when I try it on a
live one, it don't work. But I
am death on dead ones."

His favorite mount on the Santa Monica ranch was a flaky roan he
called Soapsuds, whom he had gotten from rancher friends in West
Texas. Betty remembered that their children laughed at the horse's
looks when Will first brought him home, and they had to be reminded
by their father that it was not what a horse looked liked that was important but rather what he could do. Will used Soapsuds for everything
from roping and trail riding to practicing rope tricks. The horse was
later immortalized with Will in a heroic-sized statue by Electra Wag-
goner titled, "Into the Sunset."

Betty often rode horseback with her husband in the mountains and
also enjoyed driving with him in their car through the surrounding
countryside. Being the horseman that he was, she said that he "drove a
car like he rode a horse and could usually make it do what he wanted."

Will was also devoted to airplane travel, taking his first flight in
1915. He frequently flew with fellow Oklahoman Wiley Post, who in
August of 1935 planned a long distance flight across Alaska, the Bering
Sea, and Siberia. Will took a break from movie work to fly with him.

Prior to flying to Seattle to meet Post, Will spent a pleasant day
on the ranch riding in the mountains with Betty. Once in Alaska, he
and Post spent several days flying over the wilderness before heading
to Point Barrow on August 15th to meet a friend. Before they reached
their destination, Post set the plane down on an inlet in order to get his
bearings in the fog. When he took to the air again, however, the plane
inexplicably stalled and crashed, killing the two men instantly.

Will Rogers' death sent shock waves across the United States. Americans had lost a great friend, but he was not forgotten. Today there are
airports, highways, rodeo grounds, schools, and parks commemorat-

ing his name. In 1938 the Will Rogers Memorial was established in his honor by the State of Oklahoma at Claremore, where visitors can view art and artifacts pertaining to his life. Similarly, his Santa Monica Ranch is preserved by the State of California as the Will Rogers State Historic Park. In 1952 Will Rogers, Jr., played his father in the motion picture, *The Story of Will Rogers*.

Annie Oakley

"Aim at a high mark and you will hit it. No, not the first time, not the second time, and maybe not the third. But keep on aiming and keep on shooting, for only practice will make you perfect. Eventually, you'll hit the bull's eye of success."

At the height of her career as a sharpshooter with Buffalo Bill Cody's Wild West Show, Annie Oakley was one of the most famous women in the United States. Her skill with rifle, shotgun, and pistol was unequalled by any other performer of the day, and in spite of excelling at what was considered a man's sport, she was admired for her refined and ladylike manner.

Although she embodied the spirit of the West, Annie Oakley was a Midwesterner by birth, born on a farm in Darke County, Ohio, on August 13, 1860. Christened Phoebe Ann Moses, she grew up a tomboy playing in the woods near her home. Legend has it that she shot a gun for the first time at eight years old when she killed a squirrel with one shot from her father's Kentucky rifle.

Her father died of pneumonia when she was six years old. Following his death, her mother was unable to pro-

vide for her brothers and sisters, so Annie was sent to a home for disadvantaged children when she was ten years old. There she helped take care of other children and learned sewing, embroidery, and other domestic arts.

Later she lived with a local farmer who submitted her to hard work and physical abuse. After two years of suffering at the man's hands, she ran away and eventually reunited with her mother. Old enough now to help with her brothers and sisters, she also began hunting in the woods using her father's single shot muzzle loader. Thus, she not only added to the family larder, but to the family income by trading the quail, rabbits, and grouse she killed for ammunition and groceries. Importantly, she profited enough within a few years to pay off the mortgage on her mother's farm.

Hunting honed her marksmanship to a high degree, and periodically she entered turkey shoots and other contests to test her skill. In the spring of 1881 she shot against a well-known professional sharpshooter named Frank Butler and in the match killed twenty-three live birds out of twenty-five while Butler killed only twenty-one. After the match, the two became friends and later fell in love. They married in June of the following year.

At the time Butler was partnered with John Graham in a theatre shooting act. Sometime afterward Graham became ill and was unable to perform, so Oakley took his job of holding targets while her husband shot them. During one performance, Butler struggled to hit a target, and a spectator shouted at him to let the girl try. Without hesitation, Annie picked up a gun and hit the target on the second try, and

when Butler tried to resume the act, the crowd demanded to see her shoot again. From then on the Butlers performed the act as a team.

Early in her new career Annie Moses dropped her last name and began using Oakley as a stage name. She never told why she changed her name or how she chose it, although some historians speculate that it came from Oakley, Ohio, where she and Butler frequently performed. In private, she continued as Mrs. Frank Butler.

For the next two years the Butlers played theatres throughout the Midwest at night, while Annie practiced shooting during the day. She eventually became so good that the two decided to reverse roles, and Annie became the featured performer while Butler served as her assistant. She proved to be a natural entertainer who charmed audiences with her personality, skill, and athleticism. Butler, on the other hand, relegated himself to holding her targets and managing her act, a role he later admitted he was perfectly willing to play.

Sitting Bull with Buffalo Bill

In March of 1884 the Butlers played the Olympic Theater in St. Paul, Minnesota, where the most distinguished spectator in the audience was Sitting Bull, the Lakota Sioux chief who had led the Sioux, Cheyenne, and Arapaho warriors to victory over General George Armstrong Custer at the Battle of the Little Big Horn in 1876.

The chief was greatly impressed when he saw Annie snuff out candles and shoot cigarettes from Butler's mouth. The next day he sent a messenger to her hotel requesting that she come see him. She declined, however, because she was scheduled to perform in a show that evening. Not to be deterred, the chief sent sixty-five dollars to her room in hopes of getting a photograph.

Annie later wrote that the chief's attention "amused me, so I sent him back his money and a photograph, with my love, and a message to say I would call the following morning. I did so, and the old man was so pleased with me, he insisted on adopting me, and I was then and there christened *Watanya Cicilla*," which meant Little Sure Shot.

A month later the Butlers joined the Sells Brothers Circus and began a tour of 187 cities from Ohio to Texas which lasted six months. Their season ended in New Orleans where William F. "Buffalo Bill" Cody visited the show and met them. His Wild West Show was in

Rare poster for Buffalo Bill's Wild West Show in the shape of a saddle gun case.

its second year, and because the Butlers were now looking for work, they asked Cody for a job. They were disappointed, however, when he told them that the Wild West already had several shooting acts and needed no others.

Consequently, the Butlers left New Orleans and took to the road once again. In March of 1885 they received word that the lead shooting act in Cody's show had quit, so Annie immediately wrote for a job. Cody responded by telling her she could join the show if she performed well at a trial during their forthcoming stand in Louisville.

The day the Butlers arrived at the Wild West camp in Louisville, Annie went early to the arena to practice. Using one of her favorite shotguns, she practiced by shooting clay pigeons with the gun held right side up, upside down, sometimes in her right hand or in her left.

When she finished, a man who had been watching from the grandstand walked to the arena floor and introduced himself as Nate Salsbury, the show's business manager. He congratulated her on her skill and after a short discussion hired her without consulting Cody. Annie joined the show immediately, and posters were soon hung advertising her performance.

Her first season with the Wild West was a resounding success. Audiences were amazed by her shooting skill, strength, and athleticism, especially since she was only five feet tall and 110 pounds. For her act she wore conservative dark blue or brown blouses and skirts decorated with flowers that she embroidered. To protect her legs she wore pearl buttoned leggings and topped off the outfit with a broad brimmed hat pinned with a silver star that became her trademark.

The first season's act did not dramatically change over the next seventeen years which she spent with the Wild West. After being introduced, she ran to the middle of the arena to a table that held her rifles, shotguns, and pistols. Unannounced, Butler then walked in and began throwing clay pigeons into the air, first one, then two, then three, and finally four at a time which Annie shot in succession.

Afterward, she shot targets with pistols in both hands, and then threw glass balls into the air herself and hit them with a shotgun. She followed that by turning her back on a target that Butler held and hit it by aiming through a mirror.

Her final tricks were the most difficult. For the first, she laid a shotgun on the ground ten feet from the gun table and walked to the other side. When Butler released the target, Annie hurtled the table, picked up the gun, and hit the clay pigeon before it hit the ground.

For the finale, she used a single shot rifle and five double-barreled shotguns. First, holding the rifle upside down, she hit a glass ball that Butler threw into the air. Then in succession she shot two glass balls with the first shotgun and continued with the others until she hit all ten. All eleven balls were broken in less than ten seconds. Her entire performance rarely lasted more than ten minutes. After the last shot, Annie always turned to the crowd, waved a kiss, and skipped from the arena to the applause of the crowd.

During her first year with the Wild West she toured the eastern United States and Canada throughout the summer and fall. In June Cody persuaded Sitting Bull to join the show, and Annie was pleased to renew her friendship with the chief. The chief was a popular draw with audiences who delighted in seeing him ride in the processional of cowboys and Indians that preceded each performance.

The following year the Wild West established quarters on Staten Island outside of New York City. Along with daily performances, Annie rode each day in the downtown Manhattan parade on a horse decorated with embroidered trappings. After playing to more than 360,000 spectators on Staten Island, Cody moved the show to Madison Square Garden for the winter. For this engagement Annie performed a trick horseback in which she tied a handkerchief around her horse's near side pastern and then untied it while galloping around the arena. A newspaper reporter commented that, "She (Annie) and many others believe that this has never before been done from a side-saddle by anything in the semblance of a woman."

In March of 1887 Cody loaded the Wild West troupe and its horses, buffalo, wagons, and stagecoaches on a steamship and sailed for England. The trip coincided with Queen Victoria's fiftieth year on the throne, and the Wild West subsequently entertained in London for six months, including a command performance for the Queen at Windsor Castle.

Annie was one of the show's most popular attractions. A London newspaper reported that the "loudest applause is reserved for Miss Annie Oakley, because her shooting entertainment is clever, precise, and dramatic." While in London, she rode horseback each afternoon in Hyde Park and repeatedly drew admiring comments from the Londoners who saw her. One stated in the newspaper that she "had the extreme pleasure of meeting her (Annie) a few mornings ago, and I think after watching her seat in the saddle that this little American girl is quite ahead of us."

The Wild West moved to Manchester for the winter, but the Butlers stayed in London so that Annie could give shooting lessons and perform in exhibitions. Later they traveled to Berlin and gave a private exhibition for the German Kaiser before returning to New York in the spring. For the next few months Annie participated in matches and exhibitions before joining Cody's rival, Pawnee Bill's Historical Wild West Frontier Exhibition and Indian Encampment.

The Butlers rejoined the Wild West in the spring of 1889 in time to sail again for Europe and a Continental tour that was to last more than three years. Beginning in Paris, the show proceeded to Italy, Spain, Austria, Germany, Belgium, and Holland—ending with a long stand on the British Isles in 1892. Cody and his cowboys and Indians were as popular with European audiences as they had been previously in England, and Annie, along with Cody, continued as the premier attractions.

The Wild West returned to New York in October and, after a winter off, opened in Chicago on April 26, 1893, as part of the Columbian Exposition held there that summer. The engagement broke all previous attendance and income records, and when it ended the Butlers decided it was time to find a permanent place to live. Since their marriage, they had been constantly on the road, and for years they had dreamed of having a home of their own. They chose Nutley, New Jersey, a rural community outside New York City, as the place to settle, and in the fall of 1893 they drew up plans for a three-story house. They moved into their new home in December. Being a career woman, Annie hired a maid to cook and clean her house so that she was free to work with her horses in the stable at the rear of the property.

The following March Annie performed horseback in a local charity circus in Nutley. For her act she rode into the arena standing on the back of her horse and then shot glass balls out of the air while riding astride. It was an unusual performance for her because, even though she was an accomplished horsewoman and skilled at shooting horseback,

Photo of Annie Oakley taken in 1899.

she rarely got the opportunity with the Wild West because they feared she might outperform the show's headliner, Buffalo Bill.

For the 1894 summer season Cody set up the Wild West show in Brooklyn, New York, and for the first time the show was illuminated at night with lights installed by the Edison Electric Illuminating Company. The Brooklyn location was perfect for the Butlers because it was close to their new home, and they were not required to stay in the Wild West camp. Everything was coming together for them, especially Annie's salary as she drew $100 a week that summer at a time when the average American worker only made $500 an entire year.

In the fall of 1894 Annie went with Cody and some of the Indians from the Wild West to West Orange, New Jersey, to meet Thomas Edison who filmed them with the motion picture camera he had recently invented. For her part, Annie fired a Winchester Repeating Rifle at a target twenty-five times in twenty-seven seconds and then used it to shoot glass balls out of the air. The entire segment lasted only eighty seconds.

Edison was pleased that his camera was able to capture the smoke of her gun and the shattering of the glass balls. The film was later shown on moving picture machines in New York City, giving people who had never seen her the opportunity to watch her in action.

Financially, the Wild West's stand in Brooklyn was not as successful as it had been the previous year in Chicago because of the lighting expenses. Consequently, Cody decided to take the Wild West on the road throughout as much of the United States as he could. For the next two years the troupe traveled on a fifty-two car train and performed in 300 towns and cities from Boston to the Rocky Mountains. Working at least six days a week, the Wild West often gave two performances each day. Annie loved being on the road again and especially enjoyed the stop in Piqua, Ohio, on July 4, 1896, where she performed for her mother for the first time.

Like Cody, the Butlers traveled in a stateroom built at one end of a railway coach, which was equipped with a bed, two chairs, a dresser, and running water. Despite such amenities, the constant travel began to wear on the Butlers, and when Annie turned forty years old in 1900, the two began talking about quitting the Wild West. It was a difficult decision because she enjoyed performing as much as ever in spite of the physical toll it was taking.

An incident that occurred in the early morning hours of October 29, 1901, helped them make their decision. That night the Wild West

Although train travel could be comfortable, it could also be dangerous.

train was traveling north in Virginia for its last show of the season. About three o'clock in the morning the engineer was shocked to see the headlights of another train racing toward him. Although he applied the train's breaks, he realized he could not stop in time, so he and the crew jumped before the trains collided.

All of the people on board, including the Butlers, were jolted from their beds. The first five cars hauling the show's horses were thrown from the track, either killing or injuring all of the animals on board. Most of the injured horses had to be put down. Fortunately, there were few human injuries, but the shock of the collision was enough to convince the Butlers that it was time to quit the road. Within a few weeks Butler wrote Cody and informed him that with great regret he and Annie had decided to leave "the dear old Wild West."

Nevertheless, the Butlers found plenty to do. Butler took a position representing the Union Metallic Cartridge Company, and Annie continued performing in exhibitions and shooting matches. She also starred in a stage play titled "The Western Girl."

Within ten years they attempted to retire for good, moving to Cambridge, Maryland, to settle down permanently. However, they found it difficult to give up performing. Consequently, they joined the Young Buffalo Wild West, an imitation of Buffalo Bill's show, for the 1912 and 1913 seasons. Audiences loved Annie as much as ever. One newspaper tribute read, "She has made a proud record by her wits, her activity, her genius, her naturalness, her brightness of mind, her courteous nature, and her bravery."

Afterward, Annie performed less frequently in the arena, but when she did, she often incorporated an English setter named *Dave*, who patiently let Annie shoot an apple off his head. In 1917 the Butlers moved to Pinehurst, North Carolina, where Annie devoted herself to teaching women to shoot, both for sport and protection. She was quoted as saying that it was her desire "to see every woman know how to handle firearms as naturally as they know how to handle babies." That same year Bill Cody died, and Annie wrote a heartfelt eulogy for her old friend which was delivered at his funeral.

In November of 1922 Annie and Butler were involved in an unfortunate car accident in Florida. Butler was unhurt, but Annie was pinned underneath the vehicle when it overturned. She suffered a fractured hip and a broken ankle. While spending six weeks in the hospital she was showered with well-wishes from all over the United States.

Although she recovered, she wore a brace on her right leg for the rest of her life.

Undaunted, Annie continued to shoot in exhibitions until 1925 when she developed a blood disorder. She passed away on November 3, 1926. Butler, who had been suffering from ill health, died eighteen days later. As she requested, Annie was cremated and her ashes placed in a trophy cup she had won during her shooting days. The devoted couple was buried side by side in Ohio near her childhood home.

Annie Oakley's legacy and legend live on. In 1935 her life was portrayed in a motion picture starring Barbara Stanwyck, and it was later put to music in a Broadway production titled "Annie Get Your Gun." The original show starred Ethel Merman, and it was reprised in 1999 starring Bernadette Peters. Gail Davis played Annie Oakley in a television series that ran from 1954 to 1957. In addition Annie has been the subject of many biographies, all of which reflect her personification of the finest human spirit and character. Her charm, modesty, skill, and bravery continue to inspire Americans to this day.

Tom Blasingame

In the spring of 1988 a friend called and said he was going to see Tom Blasingame, whom he had worked with on the JA ranch in the Texas Panhandle. He asked if I wanted to go along. I didn't hesitate because I'd heard about the old-timer for years from people who had worked with him, and I always wanted to meet him. He had become a legend in the cowboy world, what with punching cows for more than sixty years and still holding a riding job into his eighties. There had been articles about him in the *Quarter Horse Journal, Western Horseman, The Cattleman,* and *Cowboy Magazine.* Ian Tyson had even written a song about him. Tom Blasingame was a hero in our country.

On the day we were to go see him, we drove to his house in Claude, Texas, and got there about ten o'clock in the morning. Later, we found out that he usually only spent weekends at his house in town so he could see his wife, whereas during the week he batched by himself at the JA Campbell Creek camp in Palo Duro Canyon. Unless it was during the ranch's spring or fall works, he especially made sure he was home on weekends during baseball season so he could watch his favorite teams on television. Along with cattle and horses, baseball was his passion.

Tom's wife, Eleanor, greeted us at the door and invited us inside. She led us back to the den where the old cowboy was sitting in a stuffed chair watching a ball game. He stood and shook hands with us as we walked in. Right away I noticed the sparkle in his blue eyes and the warm smile that showed from under his trimmed grey mustache. He wasn't very tall and his legs showed the many years he'd spent horseback. He wore house shoes, but also had on the button-up Levis and red plaid flannel shirt (with the top button buttoned) that he would have worn on the ranch.

We all sat down while my friend and Tom started catching up on what they'd been doing since they last saw each other. Tom especially wanted to know about one of my friend's private mounts that he'd ridden while at the JA. He was visibly pleased when he found out the horse, now in his mid-twenties, was still alive, fat, and pensioned out at my friend's place in New Mexico.

We stayed with Tom for most of the afternoon talking about all kinds of topics, as long as they pertained to cows, horses, cowboys, and sometimes baseball. Being of a historical bent, I couldn't help asking Tom a bunch of questions about his life and how things had been in the old days. To my good fortune, he wasn't shy about telling what he remembered. He told us many memorable things that day, some of which were so good that I wrote them down the next day in order to remember them. The following is part of what I learned.

Tom said he grew up in the Indian Territory. While in school, he had trouble concentrating on his studies because he was so easily distracted when cow herds were driven past his school house. He said he clearly remembered the sun glancing off the riders' silver spurs as they rode by. As his school career was coming to an end, Tom said farmers started plowing up the country around where he lived and the "smell of the fresh dirt made me sick to my stomach." In February of his eighteenth year he saddled a big blue horse at daybreak and headed west. He eventually wound up at JA ranch headquarters.

I liked how he described the JA cowboys. He said they looked like what good cowboys were supposed to look like—big, tall, and wild as coyotes. He said they all had a wild look in their eye. He was even more impressed with the cowboys than he was with the remuda, which was the best he remembered of any outfit he ever worked for.

Tom laughed when he told how much harder he thought it was to break horses back then as compared

to today. When he was young the ranches didn't start their broncs until they were four years old, and as a result most of them pitched the first few saddles. The horsebreakers started each bronc by staking him to a log using a hackamore, so he could "rope burn hisself all over." Then the horse would be ridden for one saddle in a round pen, followed by three saddles in a big pen. Finally he'd be taken outside where a lot of them would first run away and then start pitching. Still, Tom said, most of them learned pretty quick, at least quicker than two year olds. The key to it all was that there was a lot of cow work for horses in those days, and they "rode 'em quite regularly."

The first year he was at the JA, the older punchers took every opportunity to get him to ride their broncs for them, most of which had to be eared down to get them saddled. Tom said that usually when they turned him out with a bronc, someone would throw a slicker or a hat under the horse which nearly always caused the bronc to "chin the moon."

The first spring he was at the JA he said he sometimes rode as many as eight broncs in one day. After riding so many, he was confident he would be sent with the cow outfit. But as it turned out, the cow boss wanted to see if he knew how to work before he went with the roundup crew. He did get to spend the summer with a wagon, only it was the fence crew's outfit.

The next spring, however, he did go with the cow outfit. After he had punched cows for two years on the JA, he decided it was time to see some different country and ride some different broncs. He loaded his bed and saddle and went to Arizona. He said he liked Arizona, not only because of the country, but because of how they did things there. He remarked that the old-timers said Arizona in the 1910s was what Texas was like in the 1890s, "so everybody wore six shooters and didn't think anything about it."

I asked Tom if he still rode young horses. He said that he did, adding a bronc to his mount every year. He stressed that he did a lot of ground work with them before he ever got on them, which involved first tying up their feet and then picking them up all around. After he'd saddled them a few times, he liked to saddle another horse and lead the bronc around in big circles dragging a log tied by a lariat rope to the saddle horn.

He said that his success with gentling young horses depended a lot on good halter breaking at weaning time, followed by starting the colts as two year-olds. Patience, along with getting their trust, was the most important attribute he felt a modern horsebreaker needed.

Along in the latter part of our visit, Mrs. Blasingame came in with some video cassettes. She said they were copies of movies she had taken horseback during the 1940s of Tom and the JA crew gathering wild cattle out of the Palo Duro Canyon. She wanted to know if we wanted to look at them, which, of course, we did. Tom gave us the go-ahead because, fortunately, his baseball game was over.

For the next hour Tom and Mrs. Blasingame gave us a running commentary on the cowboys and horses in the film. We saw some sure enough brush popping and slick roping by those JA cowboys. It was very entertaining, but none of it would have been possible had Mrs. Blasingame not gone out with the crew to get it on film.

After looking at the movie, Tom said the only roping he did anymore was in the branding pen. Although he said he could still drag calves pretty well, he didn't rope outside much because his arm "wasn't no account anymore."

Reluctantly, around four o'clock we decided we'd better go so we could get back to New Mexico before it got too late. We shook hands

with Tom and Mrs. Blasingame and promised to see them the next time we were in the country.

A year and a half later my father sent me a clipping from the Amarillo paper reporting that Tom Blasingame had died. The article said that on a cold day in late December, 1989, he had been out prowling horseback when he evidently started feeling tired or sick. He had gotten off his horse to rest and proceeded to pass away. The crew at the ranch got worried when his saddled horse turned up without him, went looking for him, and eventually found him where he lay.

I remember thinking what a wonderful way for a great old man to die. He'd been horseback, which was exactly what he wanted to do all his life. Few people get to cross the Great Divide with so much dignity.

Shorty Murray

I guess about everyone who has lived in cow country has at one time or another made the acquaintance of some old-timer who, by force of character, disposition, or appearance, has been especially memorable. I've known several such people myself, but probably no one more notable than Shorty Murray.

Actually, I'd heard about Shorty long before I met him. It seemed everyone around Cimarron, New Mexico, had a story about Shorty or at least a description of him. Almost everyone commented about what a good hand he was, a cowboy's cowboy as it were. They all seemed amazed at the immense size of the hats and spurs that he wore in spite

Shorty on the left at Ring Place in 1921.

of his small stature. Some said he'd never married, while others claimed that he had, although no one ever remembered seeing his wife. Typical of other cowpunchers, in his youth he was known for taking advantage of his infrequent visits to town. After roundups or at Christmas he was invariably found sharing drinks with friends at the Blue Eagle Saloon or singing cowboy songs on some street corner. Sometimes he did both. Nonetheless, everyone spoke fondly of him and said that his face always carried a smile. He was described as a little man with a big heart possessed of a cowboy's affection for kids and animals of all kinds.

I didn't meet Shorty until about fifteen years ago when I saw him at a CS Ranch branding that I had been invited to. He was in his late seventies at the time and still had a riding job with the ranch. I had just finished dragging the last bunch of calves when I was introduced to him. Since I had heard so much about him, I took a spot by him while we held herd just to see what he had to say.

We hit it off right from the start, and with only a little prompting he began to tell me almost his whole life story. He had grown up in the Cimarron country, although he had left while still young to punch cows in Nevada. Like many before him and since, he'd left because he thought he needed to see some different country and ride some new broncs. Although he didn't quite savvy the long ropes and the "dally welta" that he saw there, he had liked the country and the people he

rode with. Still, he eventually got lonesome for the mountains and canyons of his native range and decided to come home, never to leave again.

After almost everything had mothered-up that morning and we had turned the bunch loose, we rode to the cook house at Crow Creek for dinner. We sat down to the unvarying noon menu served there: roast beef, green chile stew, red chile, fried potatoes, frijoles, and tortillas and continued our visit. I learned that Shorty, whose given name was George, had worked for most of the big outfits around Cimarron, including the Chases, Philmont, and the U Bars. He said he'd always taken camp jobs in the mountains because he liked to work alone and frankly hated it on the flats. At the time, he was taking care of eight hundred CS cows on summer country at the Stubblefield camp located almost to the Colorado line.

That's where I went to see him in July later that year. The camp was situated in a broad valley at an elevation of about 8,500 feet which was rimmed by big stands of Ponderosa pine and Douglas fir. There was a good, clear creek running through the horse trap. The camp consisted of a couple of pens fashioned out of peeled fir poles and a solid two room V-notched log cabin made from the same timber. Inside, the cabin had two bunks, a Home Comfort stove, a table, two chairs and a piece of a broken mirror. The only attempt at decoration that I could see was a few old and outdated Frank Hoffman cowboy calendars that hung on the walls.

On one side by the door Shorty kept his saddle along with the few bridles that he used. His leggins hung behind the door. The cabin furnishings were made complete with a metal barrel filled with oats for his horses and a couple of sacks of salt that he packed to his cows.

I arrived in the late afternoon to find that Shorty had already returned from prowling his cows. He greeted me on the porch and told me to unroll my bed on the empty bunk. He then went to mixing up sourdough for biscuits.

Shorty Murray, Philmont Ranch c.1935

I watched as he worked and wondered why he was building such a big batch given the fact that he said he didn't expect anybody else for supper. After we ate I found out why.

His horses had come to the back door of the cabin, and Shorty stepped out and proceeded to give each one of his pets two biscuits apiece. He rubbed their foreheads awhile and then sent them on their way to poke around camp and get a drink before they went back to grazing.

After we finished eating and had washed the dishes, we sat on the front porch and thumbed through some magazines and old saddle cat-

alogs that he had laying around. He had taken off his riding boots and slipped into his house shoes. I use the term loosely because his house shoes consisted of last year's pair of Paul Bond's with the tops and heels cut off. But, like he told me, when you've got a pair of boots that fit right, you don't throw them away just because they've got some age.

Early the next morning he called up his horses. Because he couldn't see too well, he had sheep bells strapped on a few of them so he could tell what part of the horse trap they were in. All six of them were good, gentle old campaigners who had seen their share of spring and fall works, but that were still a long way from being pensioned out.

After we had caught what we were going to ride, I watched Shorty drag out his saddle. It was a reasonably new Hamley. When I inquired, he said he'd ridden Hamleys all of his life and still ordered them through the mail like he had fifty years ago. He was emphatic when he said he didn't think there was a better rig made. I remembered how Jiggs Porter at the CS had told me about Shorty's devotion to the Hamley company. He said that as far as he knew everything Shorty had ever owned, including his toothpicks, had come out of the Hamley catalog. Perhaps something of an overstatement, but I had noticed that Shorty was pictured in several of the old Hamley catalogs I had seen the night before along with several testimonial letters he'd written stating how much he liked the company's saddles.

After a few days of riding with him, I rolled my bed and didn't see him again until the next winter when I ran into him at the laundromat in Cimarron. He was in the middle of his usual Sunday routine that called for a trip to town for a plate of enchiladas at the Idle Hour Cafe followed by a session of washing clothes. While his clothes were drying, I sat and talked with him about the fall work that had just passed. When the clothes were done, he folded them neatly, but then shoved them into a brown paper sack to take them back to the ranch. I noticed that what he washed was simply another set of what he had on, being a pair of button-up Levis, long johns, a Pendleton wool shirt, a black neck rag, a white handkerchief, and a pair of socks. Typical of many bachelor cowboys, he generally wore the same clothes all week, changing into clean ones each Sunday morning.

Since those days, I dropped in on him at the ranch or visited with him in town whenever I could. Not only was it pleasant to pass a few hours with him, but it seemed that at each meeting I always picked up some piece of local cowboy history or lore that I found pertinent to the

present day. I was his student, and he never even knew it.

Shorty's gone now and, although I guess he never did anything that would make him famous, to me he was one of the heroes of this country. He was just an honest cowpuncher who always took good care of his cows and horses. I'll always remember his smile and what I learned from him, and I'm better for having known him.

Jiggs Porter

Years ago I used to help the CS cowboys brand in the spring. When they branded at their Crow Creek headquarters on the north side of the ranch twenty miles from Cimarron, New Mexico, I'd show up in the morning at five o'clock so I could have breakfast at the cookhouse with Jiggs Porter, the ranch's long time cow foreman. He'd fix bacon, eggs, and biscuits on the wood cookstove, and then we'd sit at the kitchen table and talk while we ate.

Usually it was just us, because the rest of the crew and the neighbors had to trailer from their homes or camps and rarely got there in time for breakfast. Jiggs and I would exchange the latest news we'd heard either from town or the ranch or the ranches that bordered the CS. After we finished eating and had washed the dishes, he'd set the trash can in front of his chair, get a dip of snuff—which he referred to as "toby"—and we'd visit some more.

I liked to hear him tell about the old days on the CS and the goings on in and around the little frontier town of Cimarron. He never failed to provide me with a good story about some bronc ride, cow wreck, or saloon fight that he'd been part of or had observed. An integral part of whatever he told me was the clever wording and phrasing he used that was often as entertaining as the events themselves.

I have often regretted that I wasn't able to record a lot of the things he said and how he said them, but he would never have agreed to what to him would have been a silly and unproductive endeavor. The best I could do was try to remember as much of everything he said with the aid of as many retellings as possible.

*Young Jiggs Porter,
on KP duty at the
CS Ranch.*

Jiggs went to work at the CS on June 3, 1933. He was seventeen years old. He proved to be made for punching cows and came to excel at all of the cowboy skills whether riding bucking horses, roping saddle horses, or doctoring cattle. He was to work for the ranch for the rest of his life, except for a four year hiatus when he worked, as he said, for Mr. Roosevelt, being President Roosevelt during his service in the Army during World War II.

One of my favorite stories of his early days on the ranch involved Ed Springer, the patriarch of the family who owned the ranch. As manager of the ranch, he lived at the headquarters located five miles east of Cimarron. Although a modern and progressive cowman, Springer was slow to embrace many of the conveniences that were available at the time. For example, he didn't like talking on telephones, so he wouldn't allow one at headquarters. In order to conduct ranch business, however, he had a phone line run to the cookhouse at Crow Creek that was twenty-five miles away.

Whenever a call came for Mr. Springer at Crow Creek, the cook wrote down the message, took it to Jiggs, and asked him to deliver it. During this time before WW II there weren't many vehicles on the CS, so Jiggs would go to the corrals, rope out one of his young horses, and head cross-country with the message in his pocket.

Most CS broncs of the time were pretty salty and Jiggs' were no exception. They often pitched when first spurred into a lope, but usually by the time they got to the first gate, they had lined out pretty well. He'd then long trot to headquarters, and by the time he stepped off to open the horse trap gate, he had a sweated out mount that had been traveling easily for quite a few miles.

After Jiggs delivered the message, he and his horse both got a drink at the windmill and retraced their steps to Crow Creek. It was trips like this that caused him to say that tired horses and tired cowboys made the best ones.

Jiggs often said that a lot of CS horses were so trashy that most of the time the safest place to be was on their back and not on the ground. Consequently, when a man heard the call of nature while in the saddle, it was better and safer to lean over a stirrup to do his business than to step off.

Jiggs punched cows on the CS until he enlisted in the Army at the beginning of World War II. He spent most of his four years in the Pacific with the 27th Infantry Division that was comprised primarily of soldiers from the five boroughs of New York.

While stationed on a base in Hawaii, a Special Services Unit staged a rodeo for the service men. Because Jiggs hadn't been horseback in a long

Jiggs in the Crow Creek branding pen, 1946.

175

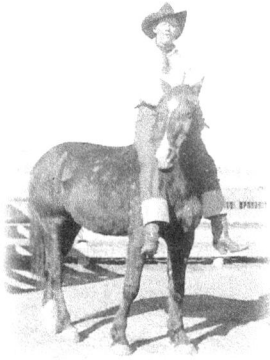

Jiggs 'horsing around.'

time, having spent most of his time riding in jeeps or sailing on ships, he was anxious to get in it. When he got to the grounds on the day of the rodeo, he noticed a man at the arena mounted on a good-looking sorrel horse. He introduced himself and told him where he was from. The man replied that he worked on the Parker Ranch on the big island of Hawaii. After they talked a while, Jiggs asked if he could borrow his horse to rope a calf. The man agreed without hesitation, knowing he was talking to a cowboy in spite of the fact that he was dressed in Army fatigues.

Jiggs stepped onto the horse, and the man handed him a rope. Putting the horn knot over the horn, he built a loop, swung it a few times and told the man it felt good to have manila in his hand that wasn't part of a ship.

After he trotted the horse to the back side of the arena and warmed him up, he knew he was mounted, so well, in fact, that he won the calf roping by beating the man who loaned him the horse. But he said he made up for defeating the Hawaiian cowboy by filling him full of Army beer when the show was over.

When Jiggs mustered out of the service, he went back to Colfax County and the CS. In 1948 he was named cow foreman of the ranch

Jiggs Porter, packing on the CS Ranch.

Jiggs in the corral, CS Ranch.

by Les Davis, Ed Springer's nephew, who was now running the ranch. Jiggs developed a great working relationship with Davis and his wife, Linda, that was based on mutual admiration and respect. Jiggs often told me how much he appreciated that they never got in the way of him doing his job, whether it was buying bulls, matching studs to mares, or shaping herds. Moreover, he taught Les and Linda's six children to punch cows so they would be able to run the ranch once they were old enough.

Under Jiggs' watchful eye the CS horse program prospered for over forty years producing big, stout colts with good heads and kind eyes. You could, and still can, do anything from a CS horse. Anyone who wanted to breed a mare to a CS stud was welcome, although it was better not to offend Jiggs by inquiring about a stud fee.

He also went around the country each year and cut colts for the neighbors, never asking anything in return, no matter how many they might have. It was a mark of the man who possessed a neighborliness that required nothing more than a thank you.

Along in the mid-1970s Jiggs started to suffer back trouble from so many bronc rides as a young man that he couldn't ride anymore. Instead, he ran the ranch from a pickup until the Davis children re-

turned from college to take over the outfit. He then slid into the role of mentor and advisor. Like any man who has devoted a lifetime to one ranch, it wasn't easy for him to step back and let the kids take their place, but he understood it as the natural progression and as it should be.

It was in the last fifteen years of his life that I spent the most time with him. During those years he'd come to my place almost every Saturday and Sunday afternoon to play dominoes. We'd play for hours, drinking beer, laughing, him telling stories of the old days and me trying to play something that would score. Invariably, he'd drag up the kitchen trash can to spit in, but my wife, Shari, never complained because she was as devoted to him as I was. He always brought a sack of candy to dispense to our boys, whether we wanted them to have it or not.

On a Thursday afternoon in his 89th year, Jiggs was drinking orange juice and playing dominoes at the Colfax Tavern when he felt a sharp pain in his chest. Several at the bar wanted to take him to the hospital, and he reluctantly agreed only after they assured him he could finish his game.

He survived the heart attack but it progressively weakened him, and he passed away in May of 2005, mourned by friends from throughout the ranch country. I was one of several who spoke at his service that was held under the cottonwoods outside the cook house at Crow Creek.

I remember saying something about how there was a lot more to the stories he told than what was on the surface. They were about hard work, caring about people, and being honest, and he never knew how much they meant to us.

The stories in this final section are fictional accounts based on events in the lives of cowboys I have known, and it's as true as I can make it to the New Mexico range.

Fidel's Rope

> "Lots of cowpunchers like to play with a rope, but ropes, like guns, are dangerous. All the difference is, guns go off and ropes go on."
>
> Charles M. Russell

The first time I saw Fidel he was riding out of some piñons near the Cerrososo Canyon branding pens. We were expecting him because John Latham, our neighbor to the south, said he was sending him over to help us brand. At the same time he was supposed to bring back any of Latham's cows and calves that might come up in our gather.

I was struck by the way he was dressed. Latham mentioned that the man he was sending was a Mexican National, but the man I saw riding a bay horse and leading a grey across the canyon didn't look like any of the ranch hands from south of the border that I was familiar with.

He wore the clothes of his native range, topped off by a straw sombrero that turned up in the back. It looked like it was of a lot better quality than the ones I'd seen in the tourist shops in Juarez. He had on a white shirt, buttoned to the top, and shotgun leggings that looked like they'd spent a lot of time in the brush. His feet were stuck in bulldog taps that showed the same kind of use, and a long grass rope hung off the big horn of his saddle.

He had a smile on his face as he rode up where we were penning cows and calves. He went directly to Tom Rupert, the cow boss, who not only savvied Spanish but was the one he needed to talk to anyway. They shook hands and, after a short conversation, the Mexican took a place in the drags to help us.

When the first set of cows and calves had been run into the branding pen, I walked over to him, shook hands, and introduced myself. He told me his name, and then I used cowboy sign language to tell him to flank calves with me. He nodded in agreement, and I could tell after the first calf was drug to us that this wasn't the first branding he'd ever been to.

What amazed me most was that no matter whether he took the front or hind legs, his shirt never showed a bit of dirt, even though he worked as hard or harder than I did. I looked down at my blue shirt, and it looked like I hadn't changed for two weeks, even though I'd just put it on fresh that morning.

When the last bunch of calves were run in, Tom told Fidel to catch his horse. Even though I was running an iron, I stopped to watch him whenever I didn't have a calf—which wasn't often because he never seemed to miss. He made a lot of long catches from both sides of his horse and caught two feet every time. It was fun to watch him.

While we ate dinner, Tom told us Fidel was going to stay with us for a few days, which suited me just fine because I looked forward to riding with him. When we returned to headquarters that afternoon, I unsaddled and went to the cookhouse to call my folks. I hadn't talked to them since we'd started to brand, and I wanted to know how their spring was going and what kind of calf crop my dad had.

After I hung up, I felt guilty as usual because I hadn't gone home to help my dad brand. But, for the hundredth time, I told myself how I wasn't ready to be a home guard and that there was still a lot of country to see before I went home.

I walked back to the corrals and as I got to the gate, I saw Fidel in the middle of the big pen doing tricks with his rope. He was making it fly and did all kinds of flips and waves that I'd only seen at rodeos. I stood watching him, mesmerized by what he was doing, before I finally walked through the gate. When he noticed that I was there, he gave me a sheepish grin, coiled his rope and walked into the saddle house.

He came back out without his twine and started talking to me in Spanish. All I could figure was that he was apologizing for wasting time doing tricks. I had no idea how to tell him that it didn't bother me in the least, and besides we were off work anyway. I appreciated how conscientious he was, but I wish I could've told him to save it for the boss if he thought he needed to.

The next morning Tom told me to take Fidel and ride Sweetwater Canyon to see how the cows and calves were doing since we'd branded. He said we'd probably take them to the high country the first part of next week, and he wanted everything straight before we started the drive.

Fidel roped out his grey horse with the prettiest houlihan I guess I'd ever seen. I was embarrassed in comparison with the loop I slopped on my colt. As usual, I justified my performance by telling myself that though it wasn't pretty, it got the job done.

I called my colt *Spark Plug* because he had a lot of git up and go, and you didn't have to ask him too hard to get it. He needed riding, like any four year-old, but he'd already shown that he could take a lot of it. I liked his disposition and felt pretty sure he'd be the favorite in my string before a year or two.

Fidel and I were saddled by six o'clock in the morning, and we rode by the cookhouse to pick up the lunches the cook had made for us. This was a major benefit of this outfit, having the cook fix sandwiches. The most I'd ever got on any other outfit was a can of tomatoes, some sardines, and a few crackers.

I rolled my lunch inside my slicker, and Fidel rolled his into a brown blanket-looking thing that he tied behind his cantle. I wanted to ask him if it was a *serape*, but I didn't know how. We took off in a buggy trot across the horse trap, and Fidel rode past me to open the gate on the far side. This made me think that etiquette must be the same no matter where you are in the cow country.

We'd ridden about two hours when Fidel motioned to the right side of the canyon where a tight-bagged cow was standing with three others. I spoke in English that I'd head her if he'd heel her. I guess I used enough sign language because he smiled in understanding, and I spurred my horse toward the cow. She turned and looked at me before she lumbered off toward the trees on the other side of the canyon.

You could tell she didn't like being interrupted from her socializing because her attempt to get away was pretty half-hearted. I headed her easily and as I turned off, Fidel came swinging a big loop with his grass rope. He picked up her feet nice and slick, and we stretched her out.

My colt sat back just right and kept the rope tight. When I was sure he would stand, I stepped off and walked down the rope to the cow. She snuffed real loud when I reached down to milk her, and I jumped about five feet in the air. It was one of those times you wished you were by yourself, and sure enough when I looked up I saw Fidel grinning at me from ear to ear.

When I had relieved the cow of her milk, I took my loop off her horns. Fidel held until I got back on my horse and then stepped his horse toward the cow so she could kick her legs out of his loop. Before we rode off, I told my bronc what a good boy he was for standing so well and decided that whenever I left the outfit, I needed to make a deal with the ranch to take him with me.

The next morning Tom asked Fidel to prowl Manuelas Canyon and me to ride Old Camp so I could check windmills. He wanted to put some pairs there because the grass had come up good. It'd been so dry the last few years that it hadn't been stocked, but the spring snow we'd had made it look like a million dollars. I took my time covering the country and rode every side canyon that had a dirt tank. It made me smile to see them full, especially since most had gone dry last summer.

I was relieved when I came to the mills in Saloon Canyon and saw their motors start when I turned them on. I didn't want to climb them, not only because I wasn't a windmiller, but I've never liked getting too far off the ground.

I trotted into headquarters about four o'clock and was surprised that Fidel wasn't there. He didn't have as big a circle as I did and should have been back already, but I reminded myself that he was a big boy and probably was just taking his time to see as much country as he could.

I didn't think any more about it and went to catch *Rocket* to reset his shoes. Fidel still hadn't come in when I walked to the cookhouse at six o'clock. I told Tom that he hadn't gotten back, and he immediately looked concerned. He said that if he hadn't come in by the time we finished eating, we'd saddle and go find him.

In another thirty minutes we were trotting out of headquarters headed for Manuelas Canyon. I kept looking ahead expecting to see Fidel ride around the next piñon, but no such luck. About five miles up the canyon we came to a park that was more or less free of trees. As we rode into it, we spotted Fidel's bay horse grazing on the far side. Tom looked at me and laughed. "Do you think he just laid down to take a nap?" he asked.

I didn't say anything, but saw that something wasn't right because the horse wasn't hobbled and he was dragging his bridle reins as he grazed. We spurred into a lope to find out what the deal was. When we got near the horse we saw Fidel sitting at the foot of a pine tree nearby. His head was bent down like he was sleeping, but he didn't have his hat on. After riding closer, we saw that his rope was wrapped twice around his chest.

Tom and I looked at each other and stepped off our horses. We walked toward him, but before we got there we could tell he wasn't just sleeping. He had a rope burn on the right side of his neck and a gash on the left side of his head that had bled pretty bad. Tom shook him, but he didn't move. We pulled the rope off him and laid him down. I felt for a pulse on his neck but got nothing.

"Damn, what'd he do?" Tom asked. I shook my head. I couldn't believe it. I'd only known him for a few days and was looking forward to getting to know him better, but now he was dead. I couldn't believe this was happening. While I stood there, Tom followed Fidel's rope to where it led under a juniper tree. When he got there, he bent down and pulled on it.

"Son of a gun," he said after a little bit. "Look at this." I walked over and saw a coyote at the end of the rope with the loop tight around its neck. It was dead, but when I touched it I saw that it was still warm. I looked at Tom and he said, "Well, his rope finally got the best of him, didn't it?"

I nodded and he looked away, up the canyon to where the sun was setting. He stood there awhile with his arms folded. When he finally turned around, he said, "Go get his horse. We better take him home."

A Sunday Ride

I was out of a job and riding the grub line, so I decided to visit Dick Champion on the Quien Sabes in the Texas Panhandle. I hadn't seen him for awhile, and I thought it might be good to check his count. I drove to the headquarters about dark. It was before the Spring works, so the bunkhouse cowboys had their bed tarps hung outside airing them before going out with the wagon.

Dick came out when I drove up. We shook hands and exchanged a few pleasantries before walking inside. There were four other men camped there, only one of whom I'd known before. The place was pretty nice for a bunkhouse with a wood stove and built-in bunks. It seemed like it might even be insulated, which I imagine those punchers appreciated especially when northers swept down across the Panhandle.

After I met the other men, we sat around the stove and talked about people we knew and where we'd been. As usually happens, they were sizing me up as I was them. Even though I was Dick's friend, they wanted to know about me in as indirect a manner as possible. But, by the time we went to our beds, we'd figured we could stand each other.

The next morning after a breakfast of fat meat, biscuits, and eggs, we went to saddle because the wagon boss wanted us to move some bulls. The studying thing started over because everybody was watching me like a hawk without trying to let on that they were doing it. They eyed me when I roped out the sorrel horse from Dick's string that he wanted me to ride. They checked out my kack, my spurs, and leggings attempting to figure out how many miles I'd been. But, I was doing the same thing to them, so it didn't matter. That's what we do.

The day went well. The sun was warm without much wind. The pasture we had to gather was pretty big, and I liked how, even though it was five miles from headquarters, they wanted to get to it horseback instead of taking a trailer. Like one of them said, why not wear out saddle leather instead of the boss's truck.

After we got in that night, being that it was Saturday, we decided to go to Dalhart to see what was there. It was a thirty mile drive, but fortunately Dick had some Jim Beam which helped to pass the time.

We went to a bar which was about what you find all over West Texas and into New Mexico. A lot of neon beer signs and a antique bar on one wall with plenty of bottles behind it. And, there were women there and not all just chippies either. Some of them weren't even ranch girls.

We started out with a few beers, but Dick decided early that since he hadn't been to town for a month and that he was going out with wagon in a week, we'd better be more serious. He snuck in his bottle, and we put it under a table off by ourselves and commenced to talk about everything important that had happened to us in the last year.

I noticed a funny thing happening while sitting there. Several women kept coming up to Dick, either wanting to hug on him or dance with him. Well, the son-of-a-gun wouldn't have anything to do with 'em. At first, I thought it was just him being polite to me, but then I saw that he really wasn't interested, which surprised me knowing what a hound he'd always been for women.

The night went on, and we talked about a lot of good things, mostly ranches, horses, cowboys, and dogs. I rode the best bucking horse during the meeting, which is how it always happens when there's nobody around to confirm or contradict what's said. I don't remember when we left or when we got back to the ranch, but I do remember we both thought we were pretty smart before we went to bed. I also remember that we didn't feel very smart when we got up.

Around ten o'clock the next morning, after we'd done the chores and made an attempt to heal up, Dick said we ought to go see his girlfriend who lived over on the LS. I didn't even know he had a girlfriend but figured she might have had something to do with the way he acted the night before. Without much conversation, I just told him I was up.

I started for my truck, but Dick said no, that we were going to ride. He said it was only thirty miles if we went by the railroad, and the ride might make us feel better. I said that'd be fine, being the kind that always liked to see new country horseback.

We went down to the barn and jingled the saddle horses. Dick pointed out a big boned, flea-bitten grey for me they called Grasshopper. He mentioned that the horse was the ranch manager's and might be a little fresh since he hadn't been ridden all winter. But he said he knew how to cover country.

After I roped him, he came up snorting with his eyes real big. Because of what Dick had told me, I didn't think too much about it. The horse stood fine while I saddled him, although he wouldn't stand when I went to step on him. But I turned him around a few times, and then he stood, and we went out the gate. Ol' Grasshopper was stout, and although I could tell he wasn't a pitching horse, I knew I didn't like how he took every opportunity to shy at stuff, be it bear grass, rabbits, or his shadow. He just needed riding.

We took out at a lope and by the time we got to the corner of the pasture, Grasshopper looked like he was ready to travel. Dick dismounted and took down the fence so we could hit the railroad right-of-way on the other side. But, the minute we rode through and Dick had tied the fence, Grasshopper started to get nervous. I discovered pronto that he was going to use the railroad track as his next excuse for something to booger at. Although I was getting tired of that action, I told the son-of-a-gun to go on anyway.

We took off at a buggy trot, when it occurred to me to ask Dick if he'd ever gone along the railroad before. He said sure he had, plenty of times, and that it was sure the best way because there weren't any gates. Then I asked, "Dick, by chance, have you ever come across any trains on these trips of yours?" He replied, "Hell, no, never."

That satisfied me. After another four or five miles, we turned off because of a bridge that went across the Canadian River. We found a gate and went down to the river. Dick said to let him go first because it might be quick sandy. I thought that'd be good because maybe it'd take something out of my grey horse. But even though we had to swim about thirty yards of sand, it didn't faze the man. The minute we were back on the railroad, he decided to swap ends with me and head north. I didn't even give him the satisfaction of cussing him, although I figured I figured I might have drawn a better mount to take a Sunday ride.

After we lined out again, we went into a big long cut in the breaks where the road went through a hill. It was about a mile long, and I was in the lead. I had my head down because the wind of blowing against us, and I was doing my best to keep my hat on. About half way through, I kind of jumped when I heard Dick cussing. At first, I couldn't hear him clear, but when I looked up, I figured it out quick. There was a coal train coming straight at us.

Now, there was no way you could sit a horse up against the band and let a train go by without it dragging you off your horse. Especially if you were riding the nice little kind of bronco I was. So, we wheeled around and lit out for Dodge. I don't want you to think that I was scared, but I sure put the steel to my pony. And that flea-bitten son-of-a-gun, full well knowing the situation, took to pitching with me about

every third railroad tie, all the while at a high lope.

Now, I'm no bronc rider, but I guess there are times when you're scared enough that you do things that you normally wouldn't do, or couldn't do. I took to riding him like I was Casey Tibbs. The train was coming on, and the engineer didn't exhibit any apparent desire to slow down even if he could have. We rode out of the cut right before he caught up with us. I stepped off, thinking for sure that Ol' Grasshopper would surely throw a fit.

But sure enough, he just stood there acting like that coal train was no more harmful than a muley milk cow. And what did the engineer do as he whipped past? The son-of-a-gun just waved at us with a big ol' smile like we were some of his best friends and that he was damn glad to see us. I bet what he was really thinking was how he was going to tell his buddies back at the railroad yard how he almost got to run down some dumb cowboys.

After we checked around and figured we were no worse for wear, we got back into our saddles. Although that wasn't all that easy for me because even my pony hadn't care much about the train, he didn't seem to think it'd be appropriate to let me get back on. Right then, I thought hard about buying him and sending him to the killers if I lived long enough.

We finally got to the LS that day, and I found out why we went. Dick wanted to announce that he and Janis were going to get married. I told them how proud I was for them, but deep down, I thought we might have gotten the work done some other way. But, like that train engineer, at least we'd have a good story to tell.

Amos and Andy

On that last Thursday of May, the boss told Lane to get his outfit and some groceries together and pack them to the cow camp in Bonita Canyon. He planned to move the mother cows to the high country on the following Monday, and he wanted Lane to be set up at the camp so he would be ready to take care of them when they got there.

Armed with his instructions, Lane went to the bunkhouse and retrieved his dishes, coffee pot, frying pan, and other cooking equipment from the back room where he'd stored them over the winter. He stuck everything in two canvas sacks and carried them to the saddle house.

Once there he put some oats in a feed bag and hung it on an elk antler by the door. He then walked to the horse trap gate and let in Joe Bird who was waiting for him along with the rest of his saddle horses. The bay horse followed him to the saddle house and waited patiently while Lane buckled a halter around his neck and hung the morral on his head.

While the horse was eating, Lane combed him. When he was finished, Lane put the halter on his head, and then picked up his feet and checked his shoes. Satisfied he had a week or two before he'd need to reset them, Lane saddled the horse and went into the saddle house to get his leggings and bridle.

"Now the chore begins," he said to himself as he bridled Joe Bird. He had to ride out into the horse trap and hunt up his pack horses, Amos and Andy. They were half brothers, both by the same stud, but out of different mares. They had been born on the same day seven years ago and had been inseparable from the moment they first came across each other. They always grazed by themselves and rarely associated with the other horses in the pasture.

In color, they were both blacks and each had a star on his forehead. They looked enough alike that the only way Lane could tell them apart at a distance was that Andy had some white in his mane next to the withers. Lane broke them as three-year-olds and had discovered that no matter how much they looked alike, they were as different in nature as any two horses could be.

Andy had been easy. He only pitched a few times and never with much enthusiasm. His brother, on the other hand, was another story. He not only broke in two every chance he got, but he was hard-headed and took three times as long to learn anything as did Andy. He was also lazy and cheated whenever he had a chance.

Because they were such partners and because Amos was the way he was, Lane decided to pack them, knowing he could always saddle Andy if he ever needed. Lane rode Joe Bird into the horse trap and looked to the far side but couldn't see the horses. He decided to ride the creek where it flowed around a mesa to a place he knew was their favorite haunt.

He found them there, standing side by side, heads to tails and scratching each other's withers. When they heard him, they cocked their heads and snorted like he was a panther from outer space. Without asking any questions, they took off in a high lope with Amos in the lead. It took Lane some riding to get around them, but when he did, they turned and trotted to the corrals like they meant to all along.

Lane turned them in at the gate but left them in the outside pen. After they finished the grain he poured for them, he caught Andy and slipped a halter over his head. He led him to the saddle house and as soon as he had him packed, he tied him to the fence where he was out of the way.

Next, he got a rope from the saddle house because he couldn't catch Amos unless he roped him. When he walked in the pen, Amos went to the far corner and put his head up to the fence to make it as difficult as he could for Lane to catch him.

The first loop that Lane threw was right on, but Amos saw it coming and jerked his head away at the last second. Lane smiled and calmly coiled his rope. His next throw settled neatly over the horse's head because Amos misjudged the loop and ducked left when he should have

ducked right. Lane thought he looked upset at himself for his mistake, but, with the rope around his neck, he turned and walked toward Lane like a pet dog.

Lane hobbled him and thought about tying up he left hind leg but let the idea go thinking he would surely stand. Things went fine until Lane started to pull the front cinch tight. Amos took the opportunity to aim his left hind hoof at Lane's right ear. Fortunately, Lane was watching, and the hoof caught nothing but air.

The situation deteriorated further when Lane hung the first pannier. At the first pressure of the weight Amos dropped to his knees. Undisturbed, Lane hung the other pannier while the horse was still down, and then grabbed the lead rope in his left hand and the horse's tail with his other. Amos scrambled to his feet because he hated to have his tail touched. Lane quickly tightened both cinches and patted the horse on the butt to let him know he didn't hold a grudge.

After Lane tied a diamond hitch over the pack cover, he left Amos on the other side of the corral from Andy and walked to his house to eat an egg sandwich and drink a cup of coffee. Before walking out, he checked his pockets for cigarettes, matches, and Copenhagen knowing he'd probably want them.

Back at the corrals, he found Andy standing fine whereas Amos had managed to get his left front leg over his lead rope. He'd scraped a good amount of hair off his leg trying to get loose, but at some point had persuaded himself to quit struggling and wait for Lane to get him out of his predicament.

As soon as Lane had Amos untangled, he tied his lead rope to Andy's tail and then hurried to get Joe Bird before Amos could do anything else. Once mounted, he rode west past the hay shed and headed for Saddle Back Ridge which still glowed in the early morning sun. He always enjoyed the view, especially at this time of year when he knew he'd be spending the summer in the high country.

For the first few miles the trail led through groves of scrub oak with a sprinkling of junipers mixed in. It was easy going so Lane nudged Joe Bird into a jog trot until the trail led up the side of the ridge. There the oaks faded to ponderosas, and they smelled sweet as he rode past.

Joe Bird broke a sweat as they climbed the last switchback so Lane pulled up when they topped the ridge. As usual, Andy stood fine, while Amos spent his time wiping his head across Andy's butt in an attempt to rid himself of imaginary flies.

Lane started again before he really wanted but thought it best in order to keep Amos from torturing Andy any longer. It was good policy to keep Amos moving so he had to watch where he was going instead of thinking about how to get in trouble.

The trail followed the ridge to its head and then crossed Fowler Pass before dropping into Bonita Canyon. Lane thought himself lucky with how well Amos had traveled so far. Only once had he fouled them up by going on one side of a tree when Andy had gone on the other.

About two o'clock Lane and his outfit were in Bonita Canyon and within a mile of the camp. He was whistling and looking at flowers as Joe stepped over a log that had fallen across the trail. Suddenly, Andy stampeded past him and jerked the lead rope out of his hand. The horse was pitching and kicking like no tomorrow, while his buddy behind was doing his best just to keep up.

Lane couldn't believe it. He figured Amos had to be the culprit until he saw some bees buzzing around Andy's tail. He looked back and saw a swarm of them coming from the log that Andy must have bothered when he went across.

Andy stopped about fifty yards down the canyon. His pack had slid to the right side, and he was kicking it with a hind foot. He soon had

the hitch loose and the pack cloth off. Having finished that work, he started bucking again and soon had his panniers empty.

Sacks of flour, beans, and potatoes along with cups, plates, forks, and spoons littered the trail for a hundred yards. When Andy quit again, he sheepishly turned and walked toward Lane, while his partner maintained an expression that professed no involvement. As Lane caught up Andy's lead rope, he stroked his neck. He then looked at Amos and said, "Well, at least he's got an excuse this time."

Audrey

Audrey woke to the clang of the Big Ben alarm at 3:30am. She pulled on a house dress and brown wool sweater and walked into the kitchen to light a fire in the cook stove. She did not have long to get breakfast because the cowboys would eat at 5:00 so that they could saddle and be at the pasture gate an hour later to start the drive.

After she filled the coffee pot with water and put it on the stove, she sliced enough bacon for Tom and his five cowboys. Next, she mixed biscuits, cut them out, and slid them into the oven to bake.

Ten minutes later she heard Tom walk in the back door. He had jingled the horses and fed them while the men rolled their beds and loaded them into the truck. She saw that he had on the blanket-lined jumper that he wore every fall. She didn't wonder because even though it was only the first week of October, there had been frost every morning for a week.

As Tom stepped into the kitchen, he told her he had broken a quarter of an inch of ice off the horse tank. "I don't doubt some of those broncs will be a little saucy this morning," he added.

He took a cup from his spot at the large kitchen table and walked to the stove to fill it with coffee. After he sat down, he told Audrey that he hoped to get the steers across McAvoy Hill at the head of Cimarron Canyon by noon. He said he would appreciate it if she could bring dinner to them there.

She replied that she saw no reason why she couldn't. Dinner meant that as soon as she had washed the breakfast dishes, she would start a roast, put beans on to boil and bake two loaves of bread. Cowboys always wanted hot food at noon, especially when trailing cattle.

By the time the bacon was done, the cowboys came in from the bunkhouse. They took off their hats and coats, but kept on their spurs. Audrey went to the ice box and pulled out a bowl stacked with eggs from her laying hens. She started frying eggs after she told the men to help themselves to coffee.

The men ate in silence, watching their table manners as well as they could, especially when Audrey came to sit at the table. When they had finished, they thanked her and headed out of the kitchen to get their hats and coats. Before they got out the door, Audrey brought the pan of left-over biscuits and told them to stick a few in their coat pockets.

After they left, she quickly cleared the table and washed the dishes. She wanted to be in time to see the men ride off in case there were any fireworks. She stepped out onto the porch right as Tom rode up on his big grey horse, Chester. He bent down, kissed her, and asked her if there was anything he could do for her before he left. "No, I'll be fine. You just be careful," she replied.

Tom spurred into a lope to catch his men who were trotting toward the pasture gate. When he rode past them, Billy Cooper's sorrel horse started pitching down the hill. It was not that the horse meant anything by his bucking, he just felt good. The other horses threw up their heads in mutual interest, but each kept in a straight line toward the gate.

Billy sat the sorrel easily even though the horse pitched pretty hard. He grinned as he pulled him up and settled him into a lope toward the pasture gate.

From her spot on the porch Audrey had a good view of the blowup. She was always entertained when the cowboys' horses broke in two, although she was decidedly put out whenever it happened to her.

As the cowboys rode through the gate, Audrey walked back into the house, thinking how different her life was compared to what she had been born to. She had been raised in a wealthy Philadelphia family and had come to New Mexico at age six when her family spent a month at the Bar H Guest Ranch in the mountains outside of Red River. She had come back every summer with them until her freshman year of college.

She liked the ranch and most of the cowboys who wrangled horses there, even though they were much different from the boys she had known back home. Over the years a few had worked up the courage to

ask her to go on rides after supper or attend the Saturday night dances.

The only one who really charmed her was Tom McLaughlin, whom she met the summer after she graduated from college. He was thirty years old and had punched cows in New Mexico since leaving his home in Texas. The last few years he had wrangled dudes because the money was better. A lot of people thought it strange he worked for wages even though his parents had a good ranch on the Canadian River in the Panhandle. But like many of his kind, he wanted to see new country and ride different broncs before turning into a home guard.

The two married a year after they met, and Tom leased a ranch in the mountains at the head of the Moreno Valley. He stocked it with summer steers, and Audrey embarked on a life as a ranch wife. She took to it immediately in spite of living conditions far removed from what she was accustomed.

Back in the kitchen, Audrey stoked the fire and started her dinner preparations. When she had a chance, she went to the bedroom and changed out of her dress into Levis and boots. She pulled Tom's two suits and some shirts from the closet and folded them, along with socks, underwear, handkerchiefs and his good boots, and put everything into his traveling duffle bag. Once the cattle were loaded on the train in Cimarron, he would ride with them to Kansas City to see them sold.

When she finished, she checked the food once again and then went out to pull the Ford pickup around to the back door. By eleven o'clock everything was ready, and she loaded the various pots and pans, along with plates, silverware, and cups, into the truck. She would have a two hour drive to Cimarron Canyon if she didn't have a flat. Before she left, she drove to the barn, got her saddle, and heaved it on top of the beds. She thought she could ride Tom's horse to hold herd while the men ate.

About an hour into the drive down the valley, she caught up with the herd. The cowboys all waved at her as she drove past, not only because they were glad to see her, but because they knew she carried their dinner in the back of the truck. As she waved back at them, she struck a big rock in the road that bounced the pots and pans. She decided she had better pay attention to her driving so as not to spill their lunch and disappoint them.

When she got to Eagle Nest Lake, she turned east over McAvoy Pass and headed into the Cimarron. The men would follow the same dirt road with the herd before they let the cattle graze in the open meadow at the head of the canyon.

She drove off the road to Tom's usual stopping place. After she got a fire started, she looked in the back of the truck to see if her driving had caused any damage to her meal. To her relief, everything had suffered through, and she carefully carried each pot and pan to the fire.

When she had the coffee on, she sat under a tree to read her most recent issue of *Women's Home Companion*. It was a bright, clear day although it was starting to get hot. She wondered how well the steers were driving.

About thirty minutes later she looked up to see Donny Chandler loping toward her from the top of the pass. She immediately thought something must have happened with the cattle and got up to walk toward him. When he reached her, he slid from his horse, took off his hat, and excitedly told her that Billy's horse had bucked him off on the other side of the lake.

"He landed on his head and got knocked out. When he came to, his head was spinning so bad Tom didn't think he ought to ride. He told me to come get you to bring the truck and take 'im back to the bunkhouse. And he told me to watch the food until they got here," Donny said.

As he hobbled his horse, Audrey gave him a few instructions and then got into the truck. She was not too sure about leaving the dinner under Donny's care, but she didn't know what else to do.

She drove back over the pass and on the other side saw the men bringing the cattle through the trees at the foot of the hill. She counted the riders and wondered why only two were missing. As she got closer, she saw Tom was in the drags leading a saddled horse.

When she was at the bottom of the hill, the herd was about a quarter of a mile north of the road. Tom left his spot and trotted over to her.

"I thought I was supposed to take Billy back to the ranch," she said as he came along side. "Why didn't somebody stay with him?"

"George Moses came through on his way to town and offered to take him," Tom replied. He stepped off his horse and started to un-saddle Billy's. "I'm going to need you to help us get these cattle over the pass. If you don't mind, ride my horse and I'll ride Billy's," he said.

"Well, great day," she replied. "I can't believe I get to go horseback instead of just cook."

While Tom pulled his saddle from his grey horse and put it on Billy's, Audrey got her saddle and blanket from the truck. She carried them over to Tom, and he handed her Chester's reins so she could saddle.

When they were ready, she led Chester into a low spot so that she could better hit her stirrup. Once mounted, they loped to the herd that was trailing easily over the pass.

On the other side, she rode around the herd and ground-tied Chester about a hundred feet away from her cook fire. She got the eating utensils out of the truck and had everything ready for the men after they held up the cattle. Two men stayed with the herd, and the others, including Tom, trotted over to eat.

When Tom got down, Audrey took a plate and started to dish up his food. He quickly walked toward her and took it from her. "Let me do that. You sit down and eat. I'll feed these waddies," he said. She looked up at him with smile like he had just given her a bouquet of flowers.

"Well, how nice you are," she said as she took the plate and a cup of coffee over to her spot under the tree.

Tom replied, "Besides, honey, you're going to need your nourishment because I'd like for you to help us finish the drive. And, oh, by the way, what would you say about going with me to sell these cattle?"

Audrey almost dropped her plate. Of course, she would want to go and immediately thought about dinners, dancing, and shopping in nice stores. But she also could not help thinking about the chores back at the ranch. Besides, she did not have any clothes to wear. As enticing as the idea was, it just was not part of the plan.

Before she had opportunity to outline why she should not go, Tom raised his hand and said, "I know what you're thinking. The boys can take care of the ranch, and I'll buy you some traveling clothes in town before we ship. And you'n get plenty more when we get to the city."

A smile brightened her face, and she thought, Maybe I'm not going to have to feed chickens everyday for the rest of my life after all.

Donnie

I always got a big kick out of Donnie. To look at him, you'd think he'd been transported by a time machine. He always wore a white shirt, button-up Levis, suspenders, wire-rimmed glasses, and high-top Paul Bond boots.

He was twenty-seven when I met him, and I found out quick that his goal in life was to dress and do his work like in the old days. His inspiration was Judd Knight, who had been pensioned out by the ranch where we were working. Judd was over eighty, but still active, running errands or doing odd jobs for the cow boss. He even got horseback every once in a while, riding two old campaigners that he'd broke years before.

Judd lived in the headquarters bunkhouse in a room by himself. He'd worked on the ranch since he was sixteen, except for, as he said, the time he'd worked for Mr. Roosevelt in World War II. He was a talkative sort and had an interesting way of telling stories that always assured him an audience.

His most avid listener was always Donnie. Whenever he could, whether at the cookhouse, the bunkhouse, or the bar in town, Donnie would be next to Judd, quizzing him about the old days. A lot of times he had to pay for the privilege by playing dominoes, which went okay as long as he paid attention because Judd didn't have patience for people who didn't play as fast as he did.

One thing that Donnie picked up from talking with Judd was the use of Navajo saddle blankets. Judd told him that when he was a kid, all the cowpunchers rode Navajo blankets under their saddles. Consequently, Donnie was bound and determined to get one.

Problem was that when Judd bought them back in the '30s, they cost a dollar and a half, and now they cost more than two hundred. But Donnie was convinced that it'd be the punchiest thing he could do to have one so he went to Taos one day and found a thirty by sixty inch Navajo blanket that set him back two hundred and seventy dollars.

I admit I was proud of his devotion when he brought it into the bunkhouse, especially because he was only making a thousand dollars a month. I made the mistake of asking him if he was going to frame it and put it on the wall. He told me in so many words that he bought it to use it, and that was exactly what he was going to do.

The summer and fall I worked for the ranch Donnie was camped in the Manuelas Canyon taking care of six hundred mother cows and calves. Along about the end of August, the boss sent me to camp with him and help him push cows and calves out of the upper end of the canyon so they'd be easy to start down the stock drive when it came time to ship.

Judd drove me to the Manuelas. When we got there, I thought he'd turn around and leave, but he got out of the truck saying he might as well take time to whip the boy in a few games of dominoes. He went into the cabin, while I unloaded by bed, saddle, groceries, and grain. Donny wasn't there but we found a note saying he'd gone prowling and would be back around three.

I nosed around a little, while Judd started a fire to make some coffee. The camp sat on the north side of the canyon near where a spring ran out of a side canyon. The cabin was old but well built. It had two rooms made of Douglas fir logs V-notched at the corners. The view of the canyon from the porch was spectacular.

Inside it was hard to find anything very modern, just like what you'd expect from Donnie. In the front room there was a Home Comfort cook stove, a plank table, two benches, and a straight-backed chair. A small table stood by the door with a tin pan and a bucket of spring water on top. There were shelves on the back wall next to the stove that held sacks of beans, coffee, and flour along with bottles of medicine.

Donnie's bed and tarp were laid out neatly on a metal cot in the second room. Aside from some Charlie Russell pictures and a few calendars of scantily dressed women tacked to the walls with horseshoe nails, the only other items on the walls were some clothes, reins, latigoes, and cinches hung on pegs.

After I finished the tour of Donnie's camp, I found some saddle catalogs and thumbed through them until we heard a dog bark. Judd and I walked out on the porch and saw Donnie jigging up from his horse trap with his border collie tagging along behind.

He was riding a good-looking bay horse and was sitting a new-made, high-cantled, slick fork saddle, the kind popular fifty years ago. I did a double take as I watched him ride up. With his rigging and the way he was dressed, he looked like what I pictured Judd would have looked like forty years ago.

When Donnie stepped off at his corrals, he finally noticed us. He waved with a big grin like he was glad to have somebody in camp to talk to besides his dog, especially when he saw it was Judd.

We walked down to the saddle house to shake hands. As Donnie pulled off his saddle, I could tell that his blanket hadn't been hanging on the wall. He started talking a mile-a-minute, a sure sign of a camp man who only has his dog and horses to talk to.

He said he'd ridden over to the park at the foot of La Grulla Mesa that morning. Then he started quizzing us about things at headquarters, until Judd interrupted him and told him to quit jabbering. He said he was a busy man and had just enough time to beat him three games.

After Donnie fed his horse and turned him out, we walked back up to his camp. Donnie got out the dominoes, while Judd poured coffee. I went back to the catalogs and every once in a while looked at them playing. I was amazed with how much Donnie looked like a younger version of the man sitting across the table.

At Donnie's urging, Judd stayed for supper and also agreed to make some of his good baking powder biscuits for us. We all had a good time visiting, and I even sat in on a few games. Fortunately, Judd was in such spirits that he didn't get upset with me when I took too long to count my points.

I stayed to help Donnie for a week and then went back to headquarters. He came down a few weeks later so he could haul groceries for the crew that would help him gather his cows.

Unfortunately, I had bad news for him when I saw him, because Judd had died in his sleep two nights before. Donnie didn't say much, but I could tell it hurt him pretty bad.

The old cowpuncher was buried the next day on a hill west of headquarters. When the service was over the preacher handed Donnie a piece of paper. Donnie walked over the side to read it.

When he was through, I walked over, and he handed it to me. It was a note scrawled in Judd's hand dated six months before. It only said that whenever he died, he wanted Donnie to have his saddle and spurs and asked him to take care of his horses.

Cowboy Reading List

A collection of autobiographies, memoirs, and recollections by men who rode the western range in the latter decades of the 19th century and the opening years of the 20th. The books are listed in chronological order by publication date. Most are still in print, and many are available in e-book format.

Joseph G. McCoy
> *Historic Sketches of the Cattle Trade of the West and Southwest* (1874).
> McCoy established a stock market along the railroad line at Abilene, Kansas, in 1867 which initiated the trail drives of Texas cattle.

Charles Siringo
> *A Texas Cowboy* (1885).
> First cowboy to publish an autobiography. He later became a lawman and Pinkerton Detective Agent.

Andy Adams
> *Log of a Cowboy* (1903).
> Written as fiction, it is an authentic account of a trail drive. Range historian J. Frank Dobie commented that "if all other books on trail driving were destroyed, a reader could still get a just and authentic conception" of the work by reading it.

Eugene Manlove Rhodes
> *Bransford in Arcadia* (1914),
> *Stepsons of Light* (1921),
> *Once in the Saddle* (1927),
> *The Trusty Knaves* (1934),

The Proud Sheriff (1935) and six others.

He rode the ranges of southern New Mexico. His books are known not only for their authenticity, but for their literary quality as well.

J. Marvin Hunter
The Trail Drivers of Texas (1920).
Compilation of trail drivers' recollections collected around the turn of the century.

James Cook
Fifty Years on the Old Frontier (1923).
Range life and hunting in Texas, New Mexico, and Wyoming, during the 1880s and '90s.

Will James
Cowboys, North and South (1924),
Smoky, the Cowhorse (1927),
Lone Cowboy (1930),
Big Enough (1931),
Home Ranch (1935) and eighteen others.
He rode ranges all over the West. Known not only as a bucking horse rider, but an artist of bucking horses as well. Illustrated all of his books. Although fictional, no other writing is truer to the range.

Phillip Ashton Rollins
The Cowboy: His Characteristics, His Equipment, and His Part in the Development of the West (1924).

William French
Some Recollections of a Western Ranchman (1927).
This Englishman managed the WS Ranch in western New Mexico in the 1880s and '90s.

Charles M. Russell
Trails Plowed Under (1927).
Stories by the great cowboy artist from Montana.

J. Frank Dobie
A Vaquero of the Brush Country (1931),
On the Open Range (1931),
The Longhorns (1941),
The Mustangs (1952)
Cow People (1964).

Raised on a ranch in South Texas, he taught English at the University of Texas. Instrumental in saving the Texas Longhorn from extinction.

Potter, Jack
Cattle Trails (1935).
Trail driving tales from Texas and New Mexico.

E.C. "Teddy Blue" Abbott
We Pointed Them North (1939).
Trail driving from Texas to Montana.

John Culley
Cattle, Horses, and Men (1940).
This Englishman managed the Bell Ranch in New Mexico during the early 1890s.

Agnes Morley Cleaveland
No Life For a Lady (1941).
Life on a family ranch in western New Mexico in the 1880s and '90s. J. Frank Dobie wrote, "The best range book from the point of view of a woman yet published."

N. Howard "Jack" Thorpe
Pardner of the Wind (1941).
First to collect cowboy songs. Worked on ranches in New Mexico and West Texas.

Jo Mora
Trail Dust and Saddle Leather (1946).
Range life of the Southwest.

Ike Blasingame
Dakota Cowboy (1958).
Texan who drove cattle to the Matador Range in the Dakotas.

Fay Ward
The Cowboy at Work (1958).
Perhaps the best description of range work through the seasons and how it is done.

Ramon Adams
The Old Time Cowboy (1961).
Perceptive description of cowboy and range life.

Daniel G. Moore
A Twentieth Century Cowboy (1965).

A throw-back Arizona cowpuncher, following the old traditional ways.

Ed Lemmon

Boss Cowman (1969).

South Dakota, Wyoming, and Montana in 1880s and '90s.

Stephen Zimmer and Gene Lamm

Colfax County, Images of America Series (2015).

Pictorial history of life in Colfax County, New Mexico.

Credits

All images are from the Double Z Bar Ranch collection unless noted below. Additional photos and illustrations on the indicated pages are reproduced with the kind permission of the following sources:

A-1 Beer Prints.com, Herman Dickson: 109-111.

CS Ranch, Cimarron, New Mexico: 97, 99-100.

Denver Public Library Western History Collection:
   61 [X-11023], 135 [NS-612], 136 [NS-455].

Hamilton, W.T., *My Sixty Years on the Plains*, 1905: 30.

History Colorado Center: 24
   [William Henry Jackson Collection, Scan #20104283]

JA Ranch, Amarillo, Texas: 146.

Library of Congress Prints and Photographs Division,
   Public Domain Images: 13-14, 17-20, 23, 28-29, 34-35, 37, 43,
   45-47, 58, 60, 68, 71, 81-82, 137-142, 167.

Old Mill Museum, Cimarron, NM: 157, 159.

Omar Barker Estate, Georgia Phillips Snead: 119-120.

Philmont Scout Ranch, Cimarron, NM: 169, 171.

University of Nevada at Reno Library, Special Collections:
   86 [NC579/8/3], 88 [UNRS-P2270-20].

Will Rogers Museums, Claremore, Oklahoma: 131.